Kind Words for *L*

A deeply researched and detailed book about a highly talented and complicated artist.

> – STEVE MARTIN
> *Comedian, writer, actor, & clawhammer banjo man*

Tony Rice is the most influential guitar player in bluegrass history, but he has always been something of an enigma. This book gets us one fascinating step closer to understanding him.

> – MOLLY TUTTLE
> *Two-time Grammy Award Winner*

A multi-perspective, deep and fascinating look at the man who revolutionized bluegrass guitar. … I couldn't put it down!

> – ALISON BROWN
> *Grammy award-winning banjo picker*

I thoroughly enjoyed reading *Discovering Tony Rice*. I loved that it is presented from the perspectives of some of the prominent musicians who worked with Tony, [and who] spoke so openly and honestly about their relationship with him. Their insights about Tony help us all better understand this legendary bluegrass guitarist and singer whom we so greatly admire.

> – DAN MILLER
> *Editor, Bluegrass Unlimited*

This is a tender, fearless, honest, and meticulously researched account, told with a storyteller's direct and engaging style of writing. I am really loving it, absorbed by it, and moved by it. This is a truly great collection of stories and quite a feat of detective work.

> – AMA BOLTON
> *Poet, publisher & Bridport prize winner*

DISCOVERING TONY RICE

Bill Amatneek

Vineyards
Press
Sebastopol

Vineyards Press
web: vineyardspress.com
R85OP03/10/24
Discovering Tony Rice/Bill Amatneek – First Edition, First Printing
ISBN 978-1-928578-33-8 (Pbk) 1 2 3 4 5 6 7 8 9
ISBN 978-1-928578-34-5 (Hbk) 1 2 3 4 5 6 7 8 9

Library of Congress Control Number: 2024900857
Library of Congress Publisher's Cataloging-in-Publication Data has been applied for.

Names: Amatneek, Bill, author.
Title: Discovering Tony Rice / Bill Amatneek.
Description: Sebastopol, CA : Vineyards Press, 2024.
Identifiers: 978-1-928578-33-8 ISBN (paperback);
           978-1-928578-34-5 ISBN (hardcover)

to
Tony
and all
who love him

ALSO BY BILL AMATNEEK

Heart of a Man – an anthology of men's writings by Updike, Roth, Chabon, Andre Dubus III, Julius Lester, Tim O'Brien, and others – 2022

Acoustic Stories: Pickin' for the Prez and Other Unamplified Tales – 2013

Acoustic Stories: Playing Bass with Peter, Paul & Mary, Jerry Garcia, Bill Monroe and Eighteen Other Unamplified Tales – 2003

Tony Rice was immaculate.
— Mark Schatz

Bill Amatneck

CONTENTS

Introduction

His name was Tony Rice, and in the world of bluegrass he was a Big Man with a Big Guitar. Stories about Tony and his priceless 1935 Martin D-28 can be heard throughout the United States and in bluegrass strongholds from Japan, England, Ireland, Australia, Italy and France, to South Korea, the Czech Republic, Brazil and beyond. This oral biography is drawn from interviews I conducted with some of Tony's longest and best music colleagues. I sought out musicians because playing music with someone forges a deep and unique personal connection; you've locked hearts and heartbeats, played and prayed together, made beauty together in space and time. We'll hear this bond in the words of all who played music with Tony.

My connection to him began when we worked together in the group that recorded the original DGQ[1] album. In that era, which began for me in 1976 and ended in 1979, Tee (his nickname)[2] flogged his guitar with muscular, 25-year-old vitality.

On November 2, 1980, as a minister in the Universal Life Church, I married him to the love of his life, Leela, when he was 29. The marriage ended in 1986, when he was 35.

In October of 2005, I saw him walk off stage following a Rowan & Rice show and cancel the rest of the tour. His right hand ached so from osteoarthritis, he couldn't hold onto the flatpick. He was 54.

He played his last gig on September 26, 2013, when he was 62. Seven years later, on Christmas Day, 2020, at age 69, Tony was found dead on his kitchen floor in Reidsville, North Carolina. It was heart disease, the medical examiner said.

Tony created a new sound of bluegrass guitar with his rhythm playing, comping (accompanying), and soloing. Though he flogged his instrument to its limits, he articulated his notes clearly – a difficult duality to master.

Tony learned from the best American acoustic guitarists, including Doc Watson, Clarence White, Dan Crary, and James Taylor. To that he added his own volume, tone, attack, artistry, and expression, bringing more out of a Martin Dreadnought than had been done previously. He changed the aural texture of the acoustic, dreadnought-sized, flatpicked guitar.

Tony expanded the bluegrass envelope and, with his work on the original DGQ album, was central to creating "New Acoustic Music." This genre fuses the instruments[*] and rhythmic elements of two-beat bluegrass, the sinuous melodies, minor-key chord changes, emotionality, and virtuosic improvisations of klezmer, the bass rhythm of bossa nova, and the walking bass of straight-ahead jazz, into a new, acoustic string-band format.

Tony leaves his fingerprints on a wide swath of flat-pickers who listened to him, learned from him, worked hard to sound like him and, beyond that, to not sound like him. He played on more than 250[3] albums with some of the greatest music celebrities of his era, including Dolly Parton,[4] Alison Krauss, Jerry Garcia, John Hartford, Emmylou Harris, and Ricky Skaggs. And he played with many famous bands including J.D. Crowe & the New South, the Bluegrass Alliance, the DGQ, Rowan & Rice, and the Bluegrass Album Band. He performed and recorded under his own name

---

[*] Significantly, the DGQ did *not* have a banjo.

and under his band name, "The Tony Rice Unit."

Whatever group he was with, wherever he played, he left his audiences gasping and slack-jawed at his astounding flatpicking.

Moreover, Tony was one of the great singers in bluegrass, some would say *the* greatest. His nasalized, plane-sung voice that he pushed from his natural baritone into tenor territory, was smoothly sharp-edged, immediately recognizable, and country clean. His album, *Skaggs & Rice,* is a lesson in singing bluegrass duets. Any of a number of tunes he sang can be heard as their definitive renditions. He penned a number of instrumentals and wrote one song on his own that I'm aware of. His choice of tunes for the albums he made was part of his artistry, as we'll read string bassist Mark Schatz pointing out.

In preparing this book, I interviewed eight of Tony's music colleagues at length. They knew and understood him well, and spoke passionately. (These interviews have been edited for length, readability, continuity, and clarity.)

A number of stories I heard are not here, either because they deserved corroboration from Tee (who's singing with the angels), didn't add meaningfully to his legacy, or are better left untold.

Some folks who witnessed or heard these stories may recall them differently. I understand. We each spin our own takes and speak our own truths in the stories we tell. The folk process – how tales morph as they travel from person to person – also informs our recollection of told stories.

Having said that, I researched diligently, and believe this is largely a book of facts, truthful stories and, yes, personal opinions, mine included. It is neither the definitive take on Tony's music, nor a birth-to-death narration of his life. It's my attempt at revealing him through his musician friends' stories.

While working on this book, I tried to respect two boundaries.

The first, of the tellers' truths, and the second, of fact, were further delimited by respect for what I feel Tony would and wouldn't want known about his life, a task of faith. I didn't want to create a whitewashed portrait of him, or avoid publishing truthful stories or factual material I gathered unless they were offensive.

I started most of my conversations with the principal speakers by asking, "How do you remember Tony Rice?" This question elicited their truths, many of them surprising. With their answers, they traveled corridors of Tony's life and expressed insights that were new to me *and* sounded spot-on.

A reader of a prepublication copy, warned me that folks who pedestalize Tony may resent parts of this biography. Certainly, I hope not. Carter Stanley, Miles Davis and Van Gogh all faced difficulties in their lives. To omit mention of Tony's life challenges and how he dealt with them, how they formed him and the musician he became, would be to diminish his stature as an artist deserving of having the truth told about him. Seeing what he triumphed over in his life helps us more fully hear and appreciate his art.

As the interviews unfolded, I heard they were allowing Tony's close friends to both tell their stories about him and express how they miss him. There was no public memorial for Tony, so I hope this modest volume replaces the void many feel at losing him, and serves as heartfelt homage to Tee.

Tony and I played music together for uncounted hours in the DGQ, drove hundreds of miles shoulder-to-shoulder in a Mercury station wagon, toked bud, broke bread and swilled coffee together, shared laughs, stories, and dressing rooms, many times.

I thought I knew him.

But I didn't.

I began discovering Tony Rice as I started listening to these stories about him, and hope you do as well.

LP cover for Japanese pressing of the original DGQ album
– photo by Robert Schleifer

In 1978, the recording won a Bay Area Music Award.
Tony called it the best-selling independently produced
album of instrumentals by an acoustic string band.

First Time Ever

The David Grisman Quintet (a.k.a. the DGQ) played its first gig on January 31, 1976, in the California coastal town of Bolinas. I lived there at the time, and made a point of catching their show. The group, with Darol Anger on fiddle; Todd Phillips, second mandolin; Tony, guitar; David, lead mandolin; and Joe Carroll playing string bass, is known as the founding DGQ. Joe (may he rest in peace) was an excellent bassist – he recorded with pianist, Mose Allison – but to my ears his approach to the bass was heavily rooted in jazz. The group's feel, with Tony at its rhythmic core, had its deepest roots in the acoustic, string-band sounds of bluegrass.

Listening to Joe that evening, I thought: *I can do that.* So I tracked down Darol's phone number and hired him to play a square dance with me. After the gig Darol said, "Hey man, I've got to get you together with Dawg and us. I'll call you." ("Dawg" is David's nickname.)

A few months later I got the call to join a DGQ rehearsal and drove to the home David and his girlfriend, Janice Bain, rented on a shoulder of Mount Tamalpais. On a warm afternoon, Tony, Darol, Todd, David, and I trooped into a basement room that overlooked a manzanita-lined valley leading down to the Pacific, uncased our instruments, tuned up, and began to play.

There was a faculty of talent in that room, but you couldn't overlook Tony's guitar picking. I'd never heard a steel-string, flat-top acoustic guitar played so hard and hot. Tony was the group's engine, and he roared with complex, commanding rhythms. Tee played a loud instrument and he picked it forcefully, filling virtually every space with guitar, his guitar all over the tune, all over my ears.

Playing in this group with Tony was playing along with him, following him. His urgent, pushed rhythms – aggressive, knife-edged – led the band. His forceful comping, thrashed with a commanding right hand, was far beyond bluegrass guitar as I'd ever heard it. His solo was heart-stopping, a precipice-daring charge. He finished the tune by detonating a Lester Flatt G-run,* an explosion of sound that would have put Lester in tears.

Tee's playing was ridiculously brilliant, stunning. Shaking my head, I whispered, "Holy shit!"

Tony had rewritten bluegrass guitar.

Lessons Taught

Tee was a music lesson. I visited his digs in Corte Madera one day, rang the bell. I heard him approaching from the other side, playing guitar. He opened the door, his Martin Dreadnought† strapped on. We stepped inside as he took the guitar off and made us a pot of coffee in the kitchen. We took our javas, moved to the living room, and sat down. He strapped on the guitar and started noodling.

We sat there talking for a half hour – a nice conversation about music and life – while improvised. I didn't hear a melody or a theme, just riffing.

We talked. He riffed.

After our goodbyes, as I walked from his apartment door, he was still playing.

As mandolinist Doyle Lawson said, "I never saw Tony without

---

* This is a guitar "lick" (an oft-repeated sequence of notes, like the melody of "shave and a haircut") that ends most every bluegrass verse and chorus, popularized by guitarist Lester Flatt.

† The Dreadnought is Martin's largest, loudest guitar, the fave of bluegrass guitarists.

his guitar. It didn't matter if he was sitting on the couch in front of the television or at the dinner table eating, he was always picking."[7]

Tony had excellent hands for playing a guitar, with fine-boned fingers, he said, but strong and highly practiced. He showed us a finger exercise at a rehearsal one afternoon.

He put his left pinky (the number 4 finger) on the eighth fret of the sixth string, a C on the low E-string. Then he rapidly played that one note over and over, alternating the fingers of his left hand:

4 – 3 – 2 – 1 – 2 – 3 – 4 – 3 – 2 – 1 – 2 – 3 …

While with his right hand, he picked:

Down-up down-up down-up down-up down-up down-up …

This is easy to say, but hard to do, or at least it takes a lot of practice to do it cleanly, and clearly Tony had practiced it. His fingers moved minimally, smoothly, not flying away, his left hand easing them into place. Back and forth he hammered, *presto*, straight-eighth metronomic, precise. His speed and accuracy were impressive.

None of us picked up our instruments on the spot and tried to duplicate the feat; maybe later, in private, but not then. We knew it wouldn't be an easy exercise to execute.

Lessons Learned

Tony learned from many people. Banjo-man J.D. Crowe taught him how to tune the first string of his guitar. He related this one afternoon.

"I'd been tuning it low," Tony said. Here he slackened his high E-string a noticeable notch, saying, "I'm gonna exaggerate from where I had it." Then he said, "J.D. showed me that I was flat, that I had to bring it up."

He geared it up to J.D. pitch, where it remained ever since. I imagine that where Tony had been tuning it sounded right to him at the time, but was flat according to J.D., a judgment he heeded.

Tee took an ear-training class from Wynn Westover. Among other lessons, Wynn (an advocate of Vitamin K for curing cancer) drilled his students in singing a tritone, a musical interval exemplified by the distance between *B* and *F*. It's not easy to nail a tritone; at every class, Wynn coached his students in singing it.

Tony learned from Doc Watson, the revered American guitarist, songwriter, and singer. He learned from bluegrass guitar innovators Clarence White and Dan Crary. Tony learned about jazz chords and voicings from John Carlini. John's first work with the original DGQ, as coach and arranger, was rehearsing for David's 1978 album, *Hot Dawg,* on which the five of us had one cut.

Tee also learned from Dawg; we all did. "This shit is hard to pick," David said one afternoon at rehearsal, and he was right. The DGQ experience stretched us all. *Thank you, David.*

Tony's Listening
Outside of bluegrass, Tony listened mostly to jazz, including trumpeter Miles Davis, altoist/bass clarinetist/flutist Eric Dolphy, tenorist John Coltrane, pianists Oscar Peterson and Dave Grusin, and guitarists George Benson, Grant Green, and Wes Montgomery. He introduced the music of Danish bassist Niels-Henning Ørsted Pedersen to the band. Niels, a.k.a. "The Great Dane," walks the bass I hear in my dreams. Tony loved to listen to jazz, and aspired to jazz, but in his heart and hands, bluegrass was his true love.

Knowing the Instrument
Tee knew the guitar, and not just how to get around the fretboard, though there was that. He knew the physical instrument – the

woods, frets, structure, bracing, tuners, rosette, purfling – as well as Martin company lore. He even knew and understood the tortoiseshell pick – more about that later. I've never played with a guitarist who understood the physical instrument (especially Martin guitars), or the flatpick for that matter, as well as Tony.

And I've never played with a guitarist who played harder, more accurately, with more self-assurance and focus, or with more dedication to the instrument and the music being played.

Bill Keith
«Bicentenial Bluegrass Band»
Venus spécialement de Californie USA, pour la première fois en France

Tony Rice, David Grisman

Michel Klec'h & Dominique Paris
Northumbrian pipes Traversière en bois

Michel Haumont
Guitariste

Zachary Richard
Cajun (acadien)-USA

FEST NOZ
Dimanche 10 Juillet

Christian Seguret
Bluegrass band France

Chakir et Lancry
Country France

Bothy Band
Musique Celtique Irlande

Aristide Padygro
Groupe suisse

Vente de Billets ; Renseignements

COURVILLE SUR EURE «MUSIGRASS DIFFUSION» 25 RUE GARNOT 28190 - (37) 23.23.69
CHARTRES «LA PIE QUI CHANTE» 13 RUE DE LA PIE 28000 - 21.08.92
PARIS «FOLK QUINCAMPOIX» 26 RUE QUINCAMPOIX 75004 - 277.72.06
        «BREIZH» 10 RUE DU MAINE 75014 - 326.11.58
        «CLAMART FOLK» 140 AV. du GENERAL DE GAULLE 92 CLAMART - 630.41.20
BORDEAUX «CLAUDE FOUQUET MUSIC SHOP» 2 RUE MAURIAC 33000

BOURG EN BRESSE «LE TUB» 15 RUE TEYNIERE 01000
CAEN «SWEET HARMONY» 7 RUE PIERRE AIME LAIR 14000 - 86.41.45
POITIERS «LA TROISIEME OREILLE» 1 RUE RENE DESCARTES 86000 - 88.37.72
RENNES «DISO 2000» 5 RUE CLISSON 35000 - 30.63.17
STRASBOURG LIONEL WEDLING 11 ALLEE DU ROBERTSAU 67000 - 35.35.76
TOUR «MUSIC LOVER'S» 43 RUE COLBERT 37000 - 20.78.06

Camping Gratuit dans l'enceinte du festival ; Parking ; Buvette, repaschaud

Poster for the festival in Courville, France, Sunday, July 10, 1977

To Europe with Bill Keith

Bill Keith is one of the three most innovative banjo pickers of our era. Another was Earl Scruggs, the most influential. In 1934, at age 10, he invented "Scruggs Picking," which became the bedrock of a bluegrass band. The bumper sticker truism, "No Banjo, No Bluegrass," means "No Scruggs-style Banjo, No Bluegrass." Scruggs Picking is a technique of playing a 5-string banjo with nickel-plated steel finger-picks on the index and middle fingers, and a celluloid pick on the thumb, in a series of right-hand "rolls" – repeated finger patterns releasing a torrent of notes that *drive* the rhythm, hard.

Chronologically, Earl is followed by Bill Keith.

Like Scruggs, Bill created a new style of banjo playing that is named after him, "Keith Picking." It's a right-hand style that sees the same finger picks as Scruggs Picking, but hears the picker playing fiddle tunes, diatonic[*] melodies. The left hand darts around the fretboard, stabbing out the notes of the tune. It's not rolls-based; it's melody-based, but those melodies must *drive* the band as hard as Scruggs Picking does – no easy feat. Bill was first rate with this. He made his banjo dance.

Chronologically, Bill Keith is followed by Béla Fleck, whom we'll hear from shortly.

---

[*] Diatonic (sometimes called "melodic" when applied to Keith picking) refers to music derived from the modes of the seven note "white note scale," C–D–E–F–G–A–B, exemplified by old-time fiddle tunes. "Chromatic" refers to the twelve-note chromatic scale, which consists of all semitones, exemplified by jazz. Visit Wikipedia.com for a disquisition on diatonic and chromatic, from which this footnote is cribbed.

Bill Keith & Tony, Courville Sur Eure, July 10, 1977 – photo by François Robert

Bill hired David, Tony, Darol, and me to back him on a European tour in July of 1977. I was delighted he asked me on board. I used to pick 5-string, and Bill was a big influence on me. When I toured with hellacious mandolinist Frank Wakefield, his instrumental, "New Camptown Races," was on the set list. Bill had played banjo on a 1964 Folkways LP, *Red Allen Frank Wakefield and the Kentuckians,* the first recording of that tune. I sat for hours at a clip, dropping the phonograph needle again and again on that cut, trying to get Keith's playing note-for-note.

At the first Philadelphia Folk Festival in 1962, Bill had entered the banjo contest. The judges – Roger Sprung and Bob Yellin among them, no slouches on the 5-string – sat in chairs below the lip of the six-foot high stage, facing the audience, where they couldn't see who was performing. Each contestant trooped up to the stage to play his three-minutes worth. When it came to Keith, after picking a very few notes, it was apparent to the judges and to anyone who'd been following banjo, that A) it was Bill Keith playing magnificently, as ever; and B) he smoked the competitors *and* judges.

Like Tony on guitar, Bill had lapped the field on banjo. Patrick Ciocca was Bill's friend, our tour manager, and the guy who snapped "The Keith Unit" photo, a few pages on. He said of Bill, "He was the Joe Pass of the banjo."

It was an honor to join Keith on this tour of Courville, Gurten, Paris, Bern, Nyon, Cambridge, and London. *Thank you, Bill.*

In England, we were looking at John Holder's poster for The Thirteenth Cambridge Folk Festival where we were playing. It featured John's drawing of a 1930s-looking, slot-head Martin (if so, made in Martin's Nazareth, Pennsylvania shop), in the hands of a slyly smiling crone. "Tony, is that a Martin?" I asked.

Detail of John Holder's poster for the 1977 Cambridge Festival

He leaned into the poster, eyeballed the instrument from slotted peghead and gears, to fingerboard, inlay, sound hole, rosette, hips, shoulders, wraparound purfling, bridge, and saddle.

Satisfied he'd seen it all, Tony stood up.

"That guitar's never been near Nazareth," he said.

It was poetic. The town that the guitar hadn't been in was all you had to know.

I'll pause to say some folks, including Dick Boak, who worked at Martin for 42 years, think it is a fair representation of a 1930s Martin 0-42 or 00-42. Eric Schoenberg of Eric Schoenberg Guitars said, "It could easily be a Martin with a little bit of artist's license – a few details changed in the fingerboard inlays. It's possibly influenced by Joan Baez's 0-45."[8]

As Schoenberg pointed out, there is an issue with the inlays. Applying a loupe to the poster, I see that at the twelfth fret, the scripted last name of the poster artist, "Holder," replaces the winged, slotted-square inlay – Eric calls it the "style 45 twelfth-fret inlay" – that traditionally ornaments this space. The absence of the traditional first fret snowflake inlay is troubling. Additionally, the guitar is missing a pickguard, but then again, some Martins of this era and ilk sported pickguards and some not. Maybe the instrument looks a tad wide in the hips relative to the shoulders. The binding is also, arguably, a skosh on the wide side. Tony saw these idiosyncrasies as indicative of a non-Martin, a copy.

It turned out he was right. I contacted the poster artist, John Holder, in Cambridge, England, and asked him about the guitar. He sent me this email:

"The Martin is actually a Nelson. I commissioned my friend Mike Nelson to build this guitar and it was a beauty. The sad part of the story is that as a penniless artist, I sold it many years ago and even sadder, when I tried to buy it back later, the new owner couldn't remember having it. I hope it's somewhere being played."

It's gratifying to discover, forty-six years later, that Tony had nailed it. Yes, he knew Martin guitars very well.

Tony's Way with Words

I remember it to this day: "That guitar's never been near Nazareth," he said, with Tony-esque brevity. Tony was creative with language. He originated the DGQ band expressions, "We have been in the bidness," and "These are the good ol' times."

We had and they were.

He gave me my nickname, "Wild Bill," which I am.

Tee was the first person I ever heard call David "Dawgy," and he created the term "Dawg music." It was Tony who suggested David call his group, the "David Grisman Quintet." When he was working with Jerry Garcia, he gave Jerry the nickname, "Garcias." He nicknamed Mark O'Conner, "OMAC."

He was the first person I heard use the term "New Acoustic Music," referencing the genre created by the original DGQ album. Tony said it was "the best-selling independently-produced album of instrumentals by an acoustic string band." I don't know if that was or is so, but it's what he said.

He dubbed Bill Keith's officially named "Bicentennial Bluegrass Band" with the nickname "the Keith Unit," a name that stuck in parlance if not posters. He gave Bill the nickname, "Brains."

Sometimes he'd refer to himself as "Yer ol' dad." He'd address any gathering of musicians as "night people," as in, "Now night people, yer ol' dad here needs a cuppa coffee."

He was the first person I heard use the word "fester" to mean a bluegrass festival. "Sings like a bird," he'd say of an instrument whose tone he particularly liked. "I fergit where I am," was one of his pet expressions. Mimicking comedian Billy Crystal, he'd say, "You look mahvelous, dahling."

"Keep your eye on your business," Tony would say, meaning don't have wandering eyes if you're involved or married. (Of this imperative, Mark Schatz said, "Kind of ironic for Tony, eh?")

"I can read readin', I just can't read writin'," he said to me many times. I heard him say, "I'll take it," and "That's got the lick," again and again. Describing a venue that had an unreverberant, flat sound, he'd say, "That's dry as a popcorn fart." When the soundman got the amplification system dialed in to Tony's liking, Tee would say, "Weld it," and sometimes, "Weld it and go smoke a joint." He introduced "flogged" into my vocabulary, a word I associate with Tony's playing, as in, "Tee flogged the guitar to its limits."

He exercised some of these expressions for as long as I knew him.

à 100km Ouest de Paris
sur les rives de l'Eure

Chapiteau

Les après-midi: Jam-sessions,
Ateliers, avec les musiciens
présents.

Les matins à partir de 10h:
Concours de groupes,
chanteurs, solistes.

Dimanche, 20h:

Bal Folk -

Scene 2:

Vendredi 8 Juillet 20h30

Jacques Ernandez
Flamenco

Bill Keith
«Bicentenial Bluegrass Band»
Venus spécialement de Californie USA, pour la première fois en France

Tony Rice, David Grisman
Veillée Québécoise
Francine Reeves, Marc Perronne
Denis Gasser, Phil Fromont

Samedi 9 Juillet

Marc Robine
Dulcimer France

Ogham: les frères Molards
Musique Celtique Bretagne

Jean Louis Vincent
Auteur compositeur

Gerard Dole & Bayou Sauvage
Musique des Cajuns de Louisiane France

Poster for the festival in Courville, France, Friday & Saturday, July 8-9, 1977

Custom-made Guitars & The Man

When we toured Europe with Keith, luthiers would approach Tee, offering their guitars for him to evaluate. But he could be picky.

One afternoon, a guitar maker showed Tony an instrument he'd created: a sparkling, cherry red, solid-body electric.

Tee glanced at it, shook his head, and with Tony-typic brevity said, "It's a different instrument."

Which it is.

Another luthier presented Tee with a gorgeous Dreadnought-sized acoustic guitar of spruce top and koa wood sides. Martin has always constructed its Dreadnoughts with rosewood sides.

Tony eyeballed the mocha-toned koa, jarringly out of place, and shook his head.

Tee hadn't played it, hadn't heard it played, and didn't have to. The guitar hadn't been near Nazareth or the woods of Nazareth, and that was that.

Tony and Bill Keith at Courville-sur-Eure, July 10, 1977

Photo by François Robert

Paris Remembers

An astounding incident happened on this tour. It slack-jawed me and is burned in my memory. It's a tale of tortoiseshell picks and payback.

The Bicentennial Bluegrass Band, a.k.a. The Keith Unit
Sacré-Cœur, circa July 15, 1977
Tony, the author, Bill Keith, David Grisman, Darol Anger
– by Patrick Ciocca

The history of France's liberation by the Allies, begun June 6, 1944, on the beaches of Normandy, has fascinated me since I read *Is Paris Burning* as a young man. With vivid writing, the book dramatizes the August, 1944, liberation of The City of Light. Reading it, I became transfixed with this period of world history. This incident of the tortoise picks bound my connection to it.

These days, most flat-picks are made of celluloid. At their cheapest, music stores buy them by the gross, stamp them with their logos, and give them away or sell them cheaply to their customers. But Tony used tortoiseshell picks. The French call them "de vrais médiators en écaille," true tortoiseshell picks. They are the choice of discerning flat-pickers who can afford them and who love the unique tone they produce.

Tortoiseshell picks are made from the shell of the Hawksbill sea turtle, an endangered species. The sale of "tortoise" is banned in most countries, and the world supply has dried up as prices have spiraled. Tortoise fans actively seek out what is left of the world stash. It's an underground matter and sales go down in cash.

Tee and Dawg dogged tortoise wherever we toured. In Paris, near Les Puces de Saint-Ouen, the flea market, we came upon a gypsy band. A genuine-looking, walleyed, oud player led the group. (An oud is an Arabian lute.) He used an orange day-glow plastic flat-pick stamped with "Musique Parisienne." The guitarist, who sported a Jimi Hendrix knee bandana and three-day old shave, used white, oversized, plastic picks that he'd hand-cut from tourist credit cards. He swore to me he pick-pocketed them for that purpose alone.

The day following this disappointment, July 16, 1977, a French friend of Tony's, Marie-Paule, directed us to an address in a shabby, residential *arrondissement*. Bill and I joined Tony and

David in this day's plectrum quest, though the two of us, who played banjo and bass, respectively, did not have a direct interest in flat-picks. It felt like it might be a fun thing to do.

(Darol was off courting his wife-to-be, Barbara Higbie, age 19, whom he'd met on Bastille Day while she was busking. Theirs was love at first sight. Barbara said, "It felt especially 'meant to be' because even though we met in Paris, we were both from the San Francisco Bay Area.")

When the four of us arrived at the address, which seemed to be up a dark alley, we saw no sign on the street indicating a music store might be lurking in the shadows. We felt our way down the alley's stone wall till we came to a door. I pushed it open. In the outdraft we could smell horsehide glue, varnish, and rosin dust. The four of us stepped slowly into a dark space that felt small, though since it was unlit, we couldn't see it well.

Someone snapped on the light. It was the propriétaire, a gentleman in his late 60s. The bare bulb revealed a dozen mandolins, lutes, and guitars lining the walls, most of prewar vintage. The mandolins, the specialty of the shop, were of the Italian, bowlbacked shape. "Tater bugs," they're called down South, for the way they look.

This joint was authentic. Bill Keith and I were our French-speaking spokesmen.

"Monsieur, s'il vous plaît. Avez-vous des médiators en véritable écaille de tortue?" Do you have any tortoise shell picks? I asked him, delighted that I'd taken French in high school.

"Non. Absolument pas!"

We all understood that.

But behind him was a wall of small wooden drawers, and on the end of each he'd pasted a sample of the item that was inside. At least a dozen drawers had variously colored plastic picks, but we noticed that two had plectra that were definitely tortoise.

"Monsieur, s'il vous plaît. Qu'est-ce que vous avez là?" Bill asked, pointing at the two drawers. This loosely translates, as "What do you have there, bud?"

"Oh yes. Those are true shell picks, but not for you," he said, in French, of course.

"Not for us!" Bill asked. "How come?"

"They are all too soft for your needs," was the gist of his response.

If he was right, the gentleman had a good point. Tony had encyclopedic knowledge of tortoiseshell picks, and gave us a talk on the subject one day as we drove to a gig in Keith's orange Mercedes minibus.

Because tortoiseshell picks are made from an organic substance, each one has a different feel. The feel of the pick derives from the quality of the shell it is cut from, and the size and thickness of cut. A plectrum may be too thin or soft for an individual player (as the proprietor suggested), or too large or firm. A quality tortoiseshell pick should be evenly brown to dark brown, without any ripples, piebaldness, or light-colored veins that show where the pick will break if it is stressed.

As Keith drove, Tony pulled a fistful of tortoise from his pocket, found one with a yellow vein that ran through it, put some thumb pressure behind that vein, and easily snapped it in half.

Tony finished the job of shaping his tortoise picks with a final step. "Buff it out on a carpet," he said. Here, he took another pick from his pocket and, holding it between his thumb and index finger, rubbed each of the three sides back and forth on the van's rug, polishing the edges to shiny smoothness.

So, tortoise picks are highly individual; you don't buy them by the gross. You audition them by hand, one at a time.

"May we take a look at them anyway?" Bill asked the owner.

"But of course!" he replied.

With a flourish, he whipped out the two drawers and presented them to us at the counter. We gasped. It was the largest stash of tortoise I have ever seen. We were looking at hundreds of glistening, mostly solid-brown plectra, worth thousands of francs. Many were too soft for Tony's or David's needs, but many were perfect.

The auditioning process began while Keith and I chatted with the old man, a mandolinist himself. He seemed interested to hear we were a touring string band, and asked where we had been performing. Bill told him about the festivals we had played in Gurten, Courville, and at Nyon, on beautiful Lake Geneva.

I asked how much he wanted for the picks.

"You choose which ones you want, count them up, and I will make you a price. But first, tell me one thing. What country are you from?"

"What did he say?" Tony asked.

"He asked what country we're from."

Tony said, "Bill, you tellum w'ur 'Muricans!"

As the old man heard this – no interpreting was necessary – a tic rippled his cheek. I was sure the price had just tripled for us rich 'Muricans and lost hope for this project. So I took a walk, bought a half-dozen postcards, found a neighborhood bistro and wrote home over a sandwich and a beer. Then I found a post office, bought some stamps, mailed the cards, and returned to the shop.

They were still sorting out picks.

Finally, they chose fifty plectra each, a hundred in all. They were fully, gleefully prepared to plunk down what could have amounted to their tour wages in exchange for this find.

A moment of truth had arrived: the cost. I turned to the old man. "Quel est le prix, monsieur?"

"Combien de médiators avez-vous?" He wanted to know how many picks we had.

"Cent," I said. A hundred.

He paused. "Cent pour vous . . .? " One hundred for you?

"Oui, monsieur, pour nous." Yes, for us.

He looked right at me. "Cent pour vous 'Muricans?"

I could hear it coming. This was going to be one million francs, two cartons of no-filter Marlboros, and three pair of Levi's, extra wide.

"Yes, Monsieur," I answered. "A hundred … for us Americans."

"Pour vous 'Muricans – c'est gratuit."

My jaw dropped.

Tony looked over at me. "What did he say?"

"He said that for us Americans, it's gratis; it's free!"

"Free? Well Bill, you ask him why."

"Thank you, monsieur," I said, "but how come?"

He said, "Because in 1944, you 'Muricans, you liberated Paris, but you never charged us anything."

Tee and Dawg went back to the van and fetched a half-dozen albums they had made and gave them to the storeowner. He thanked them, smiling appreciatively, but my jaw was still on the floor. This was France's liberation history and her payback to us "'Muricans," staring at me full face.

Dawg and Tee brought their tortoise stashes home. One of the last times I saw Tony, he still had a couple of them around, in use. He pulled a fistful of tortoise from his pocket – maybe a half dozen – and pointed out the two that were from Paris. He knew every pick in his hand, its origin, when he got it. It was Tony-ish in attention to detail.

David toted his 50 Paris plectra in a wooden matchbox. Not long after we returned from the tour, he left them in the dressing room of the Great American Music Hall when we went on stage to play the first set. When we returned, sadly, they were gone.

A few years later, some Paris-bound pickers asked David for tortoise-shopping leads. He gave them the old man's address.

Arriving at the shop, they found him still there.

"Monsieur," they asked, "Do you have any tortoiseshell picks?"

"I sold them to some crazy 'Muricans a few years ago," he said in French. "I have a few left, but they are all too soft for your needs."

Saga of the Clarence White Martin

Tony played a 1935 C.F. Martin D-28 made famous by its previous owner, Clarence White (younger brother of mandolinist, Roland White). Clarence was the master of the flat-picked Dreadnought guitar in his era. He led a parallel life as an electric guitarist with the rock band The Byrds.

This guitar is sometimes called the "Clarence White Martin," following the tradition of naming an instrument after its first known owner. It travels under other names, including its Martin serial number, "58957," as well as Tony's name for it, "The Antique." Jerry Douglas simply called it, "The Guitar."

Fortunately, Martin kept excellent records back in the day and likely still does. Dick Boak, who held many positions at Martin, including company archivist and museum curator, sent me the following information and documents. *Thank you, Dick.*

Serial number 58957 was stamped on January 23, 1935 and cleared final inspection on May 10 that year. It was ordered by Kenney Music Co. in Huntington, West Virginia on May 18, 1935, along with a 000-18, and shipped two days later, on May 20.

Five months later, in October 1935, Kenny Music returned both guitars to Martin for repair. On the next page, we'll see the letter Kenney sent to Martin about the D-28 and 000-18 they were

A. M. KENNEY, PRESIDENT   J. N. KENNEY, VICE-PRES. AND TREAS.

The Kenney Music Company

319 NINTH STREET   PHONES 21930 AND 6889

Huntington, West Va.   Oct. 14, 1935

C.F.Martin & Co., Inc.,
Nazareth,
Pa.

Gentlemen:

    We are today shipping you, by express,

1 Martin Dreadnaught Serial #58957

1 Martin 000-18   Serial #57073

    Please examine carefully and note that the necks seem to be
bowed, lifting the strings from the fingerboard to such a degree that they
cannot be played successfully.

    For some reason or other we seem to be having an unusual lot of
trouble with your guitar necks and hope you will be able to discover
what is causing it and rectify the error.

    Thanking you for early return, we are,

             Very truly,

             The Kenney Music Co.,

RECEIVED OCT 16 1935

ANSWERED OCT 17 1935

Kenny's letter to Martin about the guitar's high action – Courtesy of Dick Boak sending back. Both, Kenney said, had similar neck problems.

See Martin's handwritten note about the D-28 at the bottom of the letter, saying "Neck warped. Action high." High action would plague this instrument for most of its life.

The Shipping and Repair Orders for the D-28 and D-18

I asked Boak if anyone had registered the guitar with the company. He wrote that he "checked the records and the guitar was never registered." So there is no official word as to who purchased the D-28 from Kenney Music Company, or how it got to the West Coast. But I heard a rumor this instrument was owned at some point by Paul Westmoreland (1916-2005), known as "Okie Paul."

Westmoreland, a Texas steel guitar player, joined the Okie Migration of 1929 Dust Bowl days and landed in California – first Los Angeles, then Sacramento – opening a taproom in the state capitol, where, from behind the bar, he sold beer and sang. He became a fixture in Sacramento's country scene.

Okie Paul was born in 1916.[9] So in 1935, when the Clarence White Martin was made, he would have been 19, a dirt-poor Oklahoma migrant who lived 3,000 miles from Kenney Music Company. There is no chance he bought that guitar new.

Did he acquire the Martin in 1941 while he was in L.A., at age 25? Did he have enough cash then to afford a 6-year-old Martin D-28? Maybe ... just maybe.

But in 1945, at age 29, he wrote a country hit, "Detour (There's a muddy road ahead)," for Spade Cooley. In 1951, when Paul was 35, "Detour" became a hit for Patti Page, selling over a million records. You'll remember the tune if you're of a certain age.[10]

By then, Paul, in his mid-thirties, royalties bulging his pockets, likely had enough cash to spring for a Martin D-28 that had been in circulation 16 years. If Okie Paul owned the Clarence White Martin, he was, at best, the second owner. But, as I said, I'm unable to corroborate this tempting tale of provenance. (Another temptation is to call this Dreadnought the "White Rice Martin," after its first two known owners, but that seems too stovetop-obvious.)

Here's a publicity shot of Okie Paul holding what could be a Martin D-28. To my eyes he looks to be in his thirties, and as happily mischievous as a sailor on shore leave.

Paul Westmoreland publicity photo, circa 1951
– photographer unknown

I tracked down Paul's son and asked him what he knew about his father's Martin.

He replied, "I do remember playing on it as a child. I recall Dad having the guitar well into his late seventies."

If Okie Paul had the instrument when his dad was 75, that would be 1991, long after Clarence acquired it. So the Okie Paul story is a tall tale, and a gap remains in this guitar's provenance between its return to Martin for repair in October 1935, and its arrival in Clarence's hands in the late 1950s.

There are many stories about how Clarence acquired this instrument, but in 2009, with Clarence gone, I turned to Roland White for a first-hand narrative. Roland and I were teaching at the summer camp sponsored by the California Bluegrass Association, and sat down one afternoon for a chat about this instrument.

Roland White, February 28, 2011, at the author's home

Roland White Remembers
His Brother's Guitar

"Roland, I know Tony Rice's story about the 1935 Martin D-28 your brother Clarence owned. What's your story about it?"

His response, and I have him word-for-word, was, "That piece of crap!"

Then he explained this colorful remark.

Roland said that he and Clarence – this was 1958 or '59 – cruised the L.A. pawnshops the first Monday of each month, the day the pawnbrokers tried to clear inventory by offering deals on goods that were freshly out of pawn. Nothing showed up for the brothers, so they trooped over to McCabe's Guitar Shop in Santa Monica. Finding little interesting in the showroom, they wandered back to the repair shop.

There, in a corner, standing upside down on its peg head, in pieces, was a 1935 Martin D-28. The instrument was unstrung. The pickguard had started to peel off. The top had been egregiously, perilously, sanded down.* The fingerboard had been lopped off at the high end by two frets' worth, allowing the O-hole to be enlarged, clumsily, with a knife. That oversized soundhole became the instrument's most identifiable feature. The fingerboard had been removed and taped to the neck to keep it from wandering off. To paraphrase Bob Dylan, I still can't remember

---

* In a September, 1998 interview with Dan Miller, Tony said this is incorrect, that the top "meets factory specifications for every Martin guitar, untouched, from that era." https://bluegrassunlimited.com/podcast/84-tony-rice-interview-1998/

all the worst things Roland said about this instrument. Its beat-up condition was why he called it a "piece of crap."

The brothers asked McCabe's what they wanted for the guitar.

"What do you boys want to offer?"

"Twenty-five?" the brothers said hopefully.

Glad to get this clunker off their hands, McCabe's let the instrument go and threw in the case as part of the deal.*

Roland and Clarence took the guitar home, and showed it to their dad, Eric White, Sr., who was the luthier for the family's instruments.

He took one look at it and said, "Sure hope you boys didn't pay anything for this."

The instrument's repair was beyond Eric's skills, so the brothers took it to Southern California's "guru of guitar repair," Milt Owen. Owen took one look at the Martin fingerboard that was taped to the instrument and declared it beyond salvation. He pulled out a radiused Gretsch fingerboard blank, sanded the arch flat, fretted it, and glued it in place. The whole job cost twenty, maybe twenty-five dollars, as much as the brothers paid for the instrument.†

"That's the way I remember it," Roland said.

Owen strung the instrument with light gauge strings. He told Clarence that the guitar's thin top would balloon out if he put anything heavier on it. (In that September 1998 interview, Tony said that the top did not pull up, that it was "flatter than most" D-28s typical of the '30s and '40s.)

When he got home, Clarence, true to indie-male type, put a set of Gibson heavies on it. Sure enough, the top swelled up, making the action high and the guitar difficult to play. Later on, he put medium-gauge strings on the instrument, but the ballooning that the heavier strings had caused did not reverse itself. (Tony might say that the high action was caused by the neck needing reseting.)

---

* Other stories say $35 was paid.

† $50 in 1958 is about $550 in 2024 dollars.

Clarence sells the Clarence White Martin

Clarence hung on to the guitar into the 1960s. Then, in March of 1964, Clarence married Julia Hackney. "Susie," her friends called her. He got into electric guitar around the same time, and needed money to finance buying a Telecaster guitar and paying for a honeymoon. This is where Joe Miller enters the story.

Joe was a fellow student of Clarence's at UCLA and was involved in Miller's Liquors, his family's bottle-shop chain. He was also a folkie, and he loved Clarence's ol' Martin. He'd told Clarence that if he ever wanted to sell the guitar, to let him know. In 1965, remembering this offer, Clarence picked up the phone, dialed Joe and told him he was selling the Martin. Miller asked him what he wanted. Clarence said $500.

Joe accepted the offer.

Bobby Slone, fiddler with The Kentucky Colonels, was present for this sale and mentioned it to Tony when they played together in "J.D. Crowe & The New South." Tony was a big fan of Clarence's, and he very much wanted this guitar, so he started bird-dogging Joe.

Evidently there were many Miller's Liquors throughout the state in the early '70s. Tony knew that Joe lived in Pasadena, so he phoned the Miller's Liquors on North Lincoln Avenue and Figueroa Drive and, after a couple of tries, reached Joe. Tony said he wanted to buy Clarence's guitar.

Joe wasn't using it, so he agreed to sell the instrument to Tony … after he had it appraised. Tony's story here, as I recollect, is that Joe took the guitar to a violin repairman who appraised the instrument at $300, which is what Miller sold it to Tee for. That's what Tony told me.

There are variations in the telling of this story, including the dollar amount of the transaction, which suffers periodic inflation, sometimes landing in the $500 neighborhood. We'll come upon a different telling of this tale in a moment. Do I recall that McCabe's denies they ever owned the guitar, much less sold it to Clarence? Yes, I think so.

Ron Rice wrote to say, "J.D. Crowe and Bobby Slone lent Tony the money for air travel to California to purchase 58957."

When I mentioned to Roland that $300 was less than Joe had paid for it, Roland answered, "Well, the guy wasn't using it." That is, it had no value to him.

Tony had much work done to this instrument by various luthiers over the years. As a result, the guitar is reportedly not as difficult to play today as when Clarence owned it.

I know professional musicians who own dulcet-toned, pre-war instruments they love to play, but don't take on the road. "Too much of a risk," they say. But Tee always played his 1935 Clarence White Herringbone Martin D-28 on stage while I was with the DGQ. Branded with the imprimatur of having been owned by both Clarence White and Tony, masters of the flat picked Dreadnought in their respective eras, it is an instrument beyond value. That '35 D-28 was part of Tee's voice for a long time.

The Storm of the Century

The Clarence White Martin was not played for a couple of years, and there's a story behind that.

I visited Tony and his third wife, Pamela Hodges Rice, in Florida, during the winter of 1991. He picked me up at the Tampa airport late on the evening of November 8. We drove to their home in Crystal River, on the Gulf Coast in the southern Florida. Tony said he lived right on the water, but when we pulled in it was too dark to see much of anything. They put me up in the guest bedroom.

Mark Schatz, Pam Hodges Rice & Tony at Brendalene Restaurant, Jasper, TN.
– photographer unknown

I was pooped from a day of flying and logged off instantly.

The next morning, the sound of a diesel engine coughing to life outside the window, woke me up. I thought, *OK, there's a trucker got his rig parked next door in the driveway. He'll pull out soon.* Sure enough, after he'd warmed up, he pulled out, only it wasn't toward the highway. Near as I could tell, it was toward the water. It was early, I was still dazed … so who knows? I went back to sleep.

Two hours later, I got up. Pam gave me a cup of coffee, and Tee took me around outside. We went out the living room door to a gently downward-sloping lawn. Twenty feet out, at the edge of the lawn, was a five-foot drop to water and Tony's runabout.

We walked to the rear of the house. It was on the water too, maybe ten feet from the river. Then we went around to the back of the house, the side where I'd been sleeping and where the trucker had parked his rig. It was on the water too, fifteen feet away. It wasn't a diesel truck; it was a commercial crab boat pulling back in as we walked around.

Tee's house was on a small peninsula, a spit rimmed by water on three and a half sides. Only the driveway connected it to land. At that moment of low tide, the waterline was maybe ten feet below the floor level of Tony's one-story house.

We boarded Tee's runabout and jammed towards the Gulf of Mexico. He was wearing a sport coat and pressed slacks, not exactly seafaring clothes. He drove standing up, at full-throttle, exceeding the speed limit, if there was one. Soon, the Coast Guard stopped us. Maybe the Coastie knew him, because after glancing at Tony's I.D., he let him go without so much as a lecture.

As we pulled away, again at full throttle, I asked, "Aren't you concerned about flooding here?"

Tony said, "No way, Wild Bill. It'd take a once-in-a-century flood to come up to the house." It was prophetic.

A year and four months later, in the dawn of March 13, 1993, the "Storm of the Century," as it came to be known, swamped Crystal River as it swept from Cuba to Canada. In Florida, record low barometric pressures produced a squall line ahead of a cold front that in turn produced a serial derecho – a straight-line windstorm – with wind gusts of more than 100 mph. Supercells within the derecho spawned eleven tornadoes in the state, three of them in Crystal River. The ensuing record storm surge (twelve feet at nearby Pine Island) flooded the Gulf Coast so quickly that many folks were awakened that morning by the sound of water washing into their homes.

At five in the morning, the fire department cruised Tony's neighborhood and ordered an evacuation: Get out now. Go!

Tee split immediately in his runabout, empty-handed except for his dog, Tipper. He left his guitar on his bed, Ron Rice said, thinking the water would never get that high.

But it did. Three hours later, Tony paid $60 – the amount varies from one telling of this story to another – to a shrimper in a motorboat to go over to his house and fish out the Martin. The man said the water in the living room was neck-high when he went in. He found the guitar after a few minutes. The renowned 1935 Clarence White Herringbone Martin D-28, coffined in its Leaf case, was floating in the floodwaters, a few feet above the bed.

Tony was on a bender when the storm hit. He'd been drinking, he told me – *"all night"* – and was hung over – *"probably still drunk"* – when he evacuated. He suffered guilt over leaving the Martin behind.

Tee said he got advice from the Martin Guitar folks on drying out and restoring the instrument and they volunteered their assistance. But he opted for the services of legendary luthier, Harry Sparks.

*T*ony told me decades ago that it was Harry Sparks who brought his waterlogged Martin back to life after it went boating in the storm of the century. But I'd never heard his story. How did he do that?

Harry is universally loved in the bluegrass community. As a luthier, his skills are in high demand. J.D. Crowe, Tony, Sam Bush, Jerry Douglas, and Mark Schatz had work done by him or bought stringed instruments from him. He cares very much for fine string instruments, how to repair them and set them up to produce tone.

Harry's life story is an amazement of widely varied accomplishments. As an architect, his hand can be seen in stores such as Bloomingdale's, Macy's and Home Depot, as well as casinos and hotels. He races sailboats, and joins shooting matches as a proud member of the Muzzle Loaders Association International Confederation. He hunts and fly fishes. He spoke to Congressional Committees on needs of the physically challenged. The Americans with Disabilities Act enfolds his input.

And, he picks bluegrass guitar.

At 81, Harry Sparks, living on the Kentucky side of Cincinnati, is a close observer, colorful storyteller (as we're about to hear), and avid bluegrass fan. I called him on March 7, 2022, and asked him to tell me the story of reviving Tony's Clarence White Martin.

Harry Sparks Speaks

Tony called me in a state of panic. His house in Crystal River, Florida had flooded. Fortunately I had bought a Mark Leaf case for the Clarence White guitar. That Leaf case was not under water, as so many rumors say it was. It was floating, like a boat.

But the humidity was exceptional. Everything was damp and holding moisture on it, like sweat. It was very, very, very wet and damp. And Tony called me up and said, "What in the world's name am I going to do?"

I said, "Luckily I'm leaving Miami and going to Tallahassee, and I'm going to go right through your area."

And I said, "First off, don't take it out of the case and start drying it out. It is the last thing you'd want to do; it would be a disaster."

He said, "How come?"

I said, "It would dry out too fast and split it all to pieces."

So he said, "OK" and he left it in the case.

I drove to Larry Rice's house in Crystal River, further up the hill from Tony's, and undamaged by the storm. [This was likely March 14 or 15, 1993.] We got the guitar out. It looked like if you took an atomizer and slightly sprayed dampness on it until it was sweating.

I wiped it off and looked at it real carefully.

Harry Sparks, J.D. Crowe and Frank Neat – January 3, 2019

– photographer unknown

Harry Figures a Fix

I said, "I'll tell ya what we've gotta do. We gotta take a bunch of paper towels and wet 'em and put 'em inside the guitar. That will help it dry gradually." The outside has got a finish on it; the inside does not. So we put wet paper towels in. They weren't seriously wet; we had rung them out. We filled it up with wet paper towels.

It was the wildest guess. I had to think of something quick that would help reduce the speed with which the water came out of the wood.

So we did that, and I said, "Tomorrow I want you to take it out, and put in new, damp paper towels." I had to leave and go on; I was on the road, working.

Tony did that for about three or four days. To our shock and amusement, two years later, a couple of braces got loose, but other than that there were no cracks or anything. It was an exciting experiment that worked.

I've worked on that guitar several times, including the very first night that he had it in his hands. I set it up with new strings, dressed up the frets, checked it all out.

Harry Tells a Story or Two

I'll tell you an interesting story. I went to see J.D. Crowe many times at the Red Slipper Lounge on Newtown Pike.[5]

I went in one night, and Tony* started signaling me with his head, looking toward a table. There was a fellow sitting there with enough hair for three people, and a big beard, but he was a small man. I pointed to him, and Tony nodded his head, "Yes."

So I went over and sat down and said, "Hi, I'm Harry Sparks."

He said, "Nice to meet you. I'm Clarence White."

Well, I just about fouled myself.

He's my idol of all time. I said, "What a pleasure!" We sat there

---

* Tony was on stage, playing

and listened for a while. About that time, Tony took his guitar and gave it to Clarence.

Clarence got onstage with J.D. Crowe. They did not sing a note. They played nothing but fiddle tunes for a half hour. It wasn't recorded. And I thought to myself, *What a loss.* It was ethereal. It was so friggin' good you'd have thought they rehearsed all week, and yet it was totally impromptu. It was one of the greatest nights of my life.

Break time came, and Clarence, Tony and I were sitting there at the table. And Tony said to Clarence, "You remember that ol' Bone [Clarence White herringbone Martin] you had?"

"Oh yeah."

"Is there any chance you could get it back?"

Clarence said, "No. To be honest with you, about ten years later I called Joe back. And I said, 'Joe, it's been a long time, but I'd like to talk with you about getting that guitar back.'"*

And Joe said, "You son of a bitch. You came in here and pawned me that stupid-ass guitar, and I can't pick my nose much less that guitar,† and then you hauled off and left. I thought you'd be back in a week or two to pick it up. And here it's ten years later. You can go to hell."

Bobby Slone quotes Joe saying to Clarence, "I helped you for friendship, and I haven't seen you for a year. I wouldn't sell it back to you for any amount of money." [6]

Clarence and I were there sitting with Tony, and Tony's shoulders dropped, and he looked sad. He said, "Aw man, that's too bad."

I said, "Hold it. Clarence, do you still have his phone number?"

Clarence said, "Yeah, I know how I can get a hold of it."

I said, "Tony, Joe ain't mad at you. Why don't you call him and

---

* Tony told Dan Miller that Clarence offered Joe an "enormous amount of money for that guitar, and Joe wouldn't sell it to him." see
https://bluegrassunlimited.com/podcast/84-tony-rice-interview-1998/
† I believe this is another allusion to the instrument's high action.

see if you can buy the guitar?"

Long story short, he called him and bought the guitar. The first night he played it, at the Sheraton Inn, we were all there. It was a great night in history.

The night Clarence got on stage with Tony and J.D., how would you compare his playing with Tony's playing.

[Here, Harry laughed long.]

You know the answer.

Well, Harry, that point in Tony's career was before my time with him; I wouldn't know who was ....

There's no doubt about it that Tony was one of the finest guitar players that ever lived.

Yup.

But Clarence smoked his ass that night.

J.D. never smiled when he was taking a break, but that night, the whole time he was listening and playing backup to Clarence, he was grinning like a Cheshire cat. And Tony was like a son watching a father.

Tony practiced as much or more than any musician I've ever known ... and practiced and practiced and practiced. I'll tell you who else started that way and become a monster, is Chris Thile. The guy practices and practices until his fingers look like he's had them in a sawmill.

But Tony was the same way; he played eight and ten hours a day. That's why he got so phenomenal.

Ken Landreth, J.D. Crowe and John Rice watching Harry Sparks work on J.D.'s mid-'30s flathead Gibson Mastertone with a Frank Neat neck – photographer unknown

*S*am Bush is a laughing person, jovial, joking. He picks up the phone with a joke. As an editor, I could accurately end many of his sentences with the comment, "Here, Sam laughs heartily." Sam is a happy-go-lucky guy who finds laughter in everything, a pleasure to talk with. It's hard to believe, as we're about to read, that he was once shy.

Besides founding Newgrass Revival, a band that started its own music genre, "Newgrass," he went on the road with legendary pianist-singer-songwriter Leon Russell. Moreover, he sings the most passionate version of "Molly & Tenbrooks" I've ever heard.[11]

His 2023 induction into the IBMA Hall of Fame was well deserved. Congratulations, Sam. We're all very happy for you.

In talking about Tony, Sam shows us the music life. Sometimes a gig a week – a square dance, two hours' drive away – or five nights a week at a loud bar, or a summer of festers. And he speaks of the daily rhythms we'll hear Jerry Douglas echo: going to the gig, then home for breakfast, staying up late afterwards listening to music, going to sleep at 5 AM, waking up late, hanging out, going to the gig.

Sam and other musicians who played with Tee use the word "love" a lot in reference to each other. "We loved each other. We told each other that we loved each other," he said. It underscores my belief that musicians feel and express love easily. Giving love is what players do for life, and for a living. Jack London said, "Love is the sum of all the arts, as it is the reason for their existence."

More than one musician remarked on the deep, long-term friendship shared by Sam and Tony. "They were brothers," Béla Fleck said.

Sam's time with Tony that he most vividly recalls is when they were 18 and 19 years old – carefree, out of school, on their own, playing music! "We were such kids," he said.

This was a happy time for them both.

Well … until the granuloma thing.

Sam Bush Speaks

[I dial Sam. After two rings, he picks up the phone with:]

Altoona, Pennsylvania. Go ahead please.
Is this Sam Bush?
Is this Bill Amatneek?

It certainly is. How are you, Sam?
I'm all right! I'm all right.

Did you ever notice, maybe it's only me, but I used to watch Larry King and someone was always calling from Altoona, Pennsylvania.

[Sam burlesques Larry King's voice:] "Altoona Pennsylvania. Go ahead, please."

I get it.
So, you're writing a book about T-bone?

Yes, and I'm looking for his friends and music colleagues such as yourself to tell me, who is the Tony Rice you remember?
The Tony Rice I most remember is the young Tony Rice. He and I met on September 4, 1970. I'd moved to Louisville, Kentucky after high school, and at the invitation of the Bluegrass Alliance, started playing guitar in the band, taking Dan Crary's place, playing bars in Louisville.

Dan Crary had a few more engagements to fulfill with the band, so I would go along as an extra person to play mandolin with them on the road. Well, Tony was playing in Reidsville, North Carolina at Carlton Haney's Camp Springs Labor Day Festival in 1970.

He knew who I was but I hadn't met him yet. It was a Sunday afternoon at the festival and we had a very good mutual friend over the years named John Kaparakis. John was very good friends with Roland and Clarence White. John came up to me and said, "I just heard a guy sitting out in the field playing like Clarence."

So we went over and there was the world's skinniest man sitting on a brand new, blue Martin case. He was sitting there playing someone's brand new D-45 Martin. He did play Clarence White stuff. He did sound like Clarence. So we started to talking, and I said "Man, if you come play guitar with us then I can go back to mandolin and we can have the band like that." So now I head back over to the campsite and Tony's going to come over. And I told the guys "Hey I just got this great guitar player to play with us."

And the other guys were basically, "You what? You can't just ask somebody to join the band."

At any rate, a week after he came over and played with us, he had moved to Louisville and joined us. So that's how we got it going.

That first jam session was at a campfire where Courtney Johnson on banjo had driven his own school bus down there and my dad had ridden down with him and some others from Barren County, Kentucky. And within a couple of months, Courtney became the banjo player in Bluegrass Alliance as well.

At any rate in that first jam when we were all marveling at Tony's playing, and he had the high singing voice and could play the guitar like Clarence and it was like, man, we've got to ask him to join. That was somewhere in September of 1970 we did that.

And by the way, Tony and I, on September 4, one of us would

always call the other one to say happy anniversary of the day we met. And in the last couple of years, I was afraid he was getting where he wasn't communicating very much with people. We always had a pleasant memory of that day and I may even still have a voice mail saved from one of those calls, I'm not sure.

So Tony moved up to Louisville and we started playing five nights a week at a place called the Tam O'Shanter. We went through who should or shouldn't be the emcee, and we had to finally agree that Ebo Walker would be the emcee because he was the least worst of all of us. We were all terrible emcees; Ebo just wasn't as bad as the rest of us.

We played all winter that way until our bar job went away so we actually went through that winter of 1970 going into '71 as pretty lean times. Our one gig a week for a while was to drive from Cave City, Kentucky down to Louisville, which was two hours or so, and play a square dance on Saturday afternoons. Pickings were slim.

So Tony ended up moving in with me and my first wife after not having the money to pay his rent and got locked out of his boardinghouse. I helped him climb up the window to retrieve his records and his guitar. He came to live with us for a number of months and then he got his own place again.

We always kind of wondered if Tony was going to stay very long in the band. He stayed pretty much right out a year. His last job with us was on Labor Day weekend in 1971, at Camp Springs North Carolina, just where we had met a year before.

And by the way, we actually went into the studio and cut a few sides, and I've never known what happened to them, never known where they went. One of them was a song Tony wrote called "Like a Train."* I remember that.

Tony had first given us notice that he was going to leave Bluegrass Alliance because Eddie Adcock and mandolinist Jimmy

---

* Offhand, I can't find a reference to that song on the web.

Gaudreau were starting a new band they were going to call The Second Generation. Originally Tony was to be the guitar player and they had some rehearsals and everything.

But Doyle Lawson, who was playing guitar with J.D. Crowe, was then offered the mandolin job with the Country Gentlemen, leaving the guitar chair open in J.D.'s band, whereupon they offered it to Tony. And Tony *wanted* to play in J.D.'s band with his brother Larry, and Crowe and Bobby Slone; that's who he most wanted to play with. So he went on with J.D.

At that Camp Springs Festival, Tony played with both J.D. Crowe and the Bluegrass Alliance that weekend of Labor Day 1971. There is a song by each band in the documentary that came out called *Bluegrass Country Soul*.

So you can see Tony playing with both bands that weekend. That was his last one with us down in Camp Springs. And we had a really good festival year that year. We did great at Bean Blossom. One of our highlights was to play at the 33rd National Folk Festival at Wolf Trap Barns in Vienna, Virginia.

It was like after playing all winter of '70-'71 in the bars, we were rewarded by getting to play festivals. All of a sudden this great world of festivals came to us, and we did well that summer.

Tony was with the Bluegrass Alliance one year. But he and I always stayed in touch. Sometimes a bunch of us would go over to Louisville* to hear J.D. with Tony.

One of my highlights was somewhere around of the winter of 1972 or 1973. Larry Rice had to have a cyst taken off his wrist. He had to be hospitalized for five days or so. So I ended up filling in for Larry. New Grass Revival didn't have any work for a couple of weeks, so I ended up playing Larry's mandolin because at this time J.D.'s band was plugged in with electric instruments like the Osborne Brothers did.

---

* Ron Rice suggest that maybe Sam meant Lexington, Kentucky.

So Tony was playing a plugged-in guitar, and we played five nights a week at the Red Slipper Lounge in Lexington at the Holiday Inn. I did that for two weeks and it was such a great time just playing with Crowe and Tony and Bobby Slone. They had a drummer, Jimmy Klugh.

It was a really great time. I stayed with Tony and Kate, his first wife. This routine every day: you'd go to work at about 8 PM; after work we'd go back to Tony's house – now it's one or two o'clock in the morning – and eat a great big breakfast. Kate would cook this gigantic breakfast of pancakes, eggs, and sausage. Then we'd listen to John Coltrane Records until about four or five in the morning, go to sleep, wake up about one or two in the afternoon, get up, hang around, eat, and get ready to go back to work.

I had an incredible time doing that because when J.D. Crowe is playing "Train 45," it's the moment of truth.[12] Just when you thought you were good, step up there with J.D. and Tony and try to play "Train 45."

Tony and I didn't see each other a lot once he started playing with J.D. We'd run into each other at festivals and hang out. We talked on the phone and stayed in touch.

And then the next thing I knew, Tony had moved to California and started playing with David Grisman. When that first DGQ album came out, I must have bought eight to ten copies, I was so knocked out by that record and everyone's playing and the arrangements and the tunes that I would buy them and send them to people saying, "You've got to hear this."

So it was obviously during that period when you and I would have met.*

Now Tony had been in the band and he wanted to make a bluegrass kind of vocal record, having not sung any, so he assembled

---

* We met at Arch Street Studios, in Berkeley, in 1979

us all, I guess it was in 1978 or '79, he assembled Jerry and me. And actually that's the first time I played with Jerry Douglas and Ricky Skaggs. Even though we knew each other, we hadn't played together when Tony cut *Manzanita*. And that led to playing on a couple more instrumental records with Tony. I played on *Acoustics* and *Mar West*.

And then it got to where Tony was having a band and I wasn't needed anymore to play on those records. I know how that is. You've got Jimmy Gaudreau or John Reischman or some other great mandolin players there. So I didn't record with him as much after that.

It was great. I'd go to California, and again, hang at his house and listen to John Coltrane and Miles Davis while recording bluegrass tunes, or other tunes, especially instrumentals later on that he was writing. He made up a couple. It was actually turning me on to music I hadn't listened to before, with Coltrane and Miles Davis. I'd listened to more of the electric Miles Davis but not the classic stuff Tony was more into.

What do you remember about the first time you picked with Tony?

Yeah, it was in the jam session at Reidsville around the campfire by Courtney Johnson's bus. The first time we played together, we were knocked out. Because at the time, his main style was to copy Clarence White. He knew Clarence, was a friend of his. Clarence influenced him, and he was a devotee of Clarence. And certainly at that time he was the best person I had heard play like Clarence. Lots of people were aware of Clarence White and trying to play like him, but no one had that timing as good as Tony did.

When we were living together, Tony was really funny back then. Our styles weren't realized or our singing. We were so young. I now know he was 19, I was 18, when we first started playing together, the year we spent together.

I got some great little snapshots of when I turned 19 in April that year. And Tony and I and Barry Stevens, the rock musician, a friend of ours, were all hanging out in Cherokee Park in Louisville, wearing funny hats.

But the greatest part was when – and we didn't work a lot so we had lots of time on our hands – when one day Tony would wake up and go "Yeah, let's go downtown. I feel like being a tourist today."

And I said, "Tourist? I hate to use the word 'style,' but …"

And he goes, "Tourist style. Yeah."

And of course the guy only weighed about 120 pounds. And he would put on a pair of Bermuda shorts, with little, tiny, skinny socks that only came up to his ankles, with black dress shoes on. And he had a Hawaiian shirt and a pair of Ray-Ban style sunglasses, and they weren't at all fashionable, by the way, in 1971. He had a camera, that he had no film in, around his neck.

And they used to make these little funny hats with a miniature beer can on one side, and a little church key on the other. And he'd wear that. So he called it his "tourist outfit." We would drive to downtown Louisville, and he would go around asking people if he could take their pictures and he never had any film in the camera.

It was a really joyful time for both of us, because it was the first time we were on our own, and playing music, and loving that life and the freedom to get to play. So, we were kids together.

I don't have a snapshot of him wearing the tourist outfit, but he was a tourist. The Hawaiian shirt and the madras shorts. It was wonderful. We were just having fun, cause we didn't have any money but we found ways to always have fun and amuse ourselves.

W e did a lot of playing and practicing. And I can remember, we sang over one mic, so when he and Lonnie Pierce and I were the trio singing in the band – I was basically the baritone singer – I would sing lead sometimes, but Tony sang lead on the choruses.

When we would practice and work up songs, we would have a mic stand that we would work around so you could practice the bluegrass choreography of who gets in the middle and who is on the end. The guitar player had the luxury of standing in one spot, but the rest of us had to do choreography based on who was going to take the next solo.

Generally, the guy who was going to take the next solo would probably stand in the middle. Not only would we practice our music, but we would practice how we were going to stand in front of microphones, and how we did all that.

For J.D. Crowe's band and the Bluegrass Alliance, we were all really happy when we got to have our own separate microphones. And that you didn't have to try to get up on your tiptoes, and hike your mandolin up to the vocal mic. That was a luxury. Separate mics, and having monitors to hear, that was a luxury. At the time I'm talking about, the most that Tony and I played together, for that year, in the Bluegrass Alliance, we didn't have many monitor speakers. You'd play in these loud bars and that's where you developed a really hard attack with your right hand on all the instruments. Getting separate mics and getting a monitor system was a great day for all of us.

Was this the era of the granuloma scare?

Yes, it was. Let's just say that those of us who knew him know that he could sometimes have a flair for the dramatic.

So, one morning we wake up and we're hanging out, and he goes, "I need you to take me to the clinic. I'm not doing good."

I say "What's the matter?"

He says, "I think I've got granuloma."

And I said, "I haven't heard of that."

He said, "Well, …" – and he was, again, being a little dramatic – "You get these sores all over you, and then you lose a lot of weight … right before you die. And I've lost a lot of weight lately."

I said, "Well, yeah. I'll take you to the health clinic down there."

So we drive down there, and he's pretty worried, and he goes in, and I sit out in the car and read the paper. He was in there a couple of hours, ya know, by the time it takes to get in.

All of a sudden, I see the door burst open, and he comes out and he's got more of a spring to his step, got a little smile on his face, he's looking a little better, and I say,

"Well, what's going on? Do you have granuloma?"

He said, "No, it's not granuloma. It's acne."

"And what's your prescription?"

He said, "It's Dial soap."

[*We enjoy a long laugh here.*]

As it turned out, he wasn't about to die after all. He had acne, and some people, if you have it pretty good … He had it on his back and things, which actually would also keep you from being drafted into the army, by the way. I think his classification was 1-Y.* After examining him, he wasn't gonna be one of the first ones they wanted in the army. So his granuloma, or acne as it was later called, was what kept him out of the army.

Apparently, before he joined Bluegrass Alliance, he tried to join the Navy. The Navy didn't want him because he was color blind,[13] which might explain some of his wardrobes in years later.

The army didn't care if you were color blind. They would have taken him.

Me, I got a high lottery number. I never had to go through that as much as Tony did. But you sure stayed worried about the

---

* Ron Rice wrote, "Tony was classified as 4-F because of his broken nose. Larry accidentally broke Tony's nose while playing on a bunk bed."

thought of having to go to Vietnam. And I know that in my case, at my height, if I weighed under 121, I'd be underweight. So on purpose I stayed at 130 pounds, so if I got my notice I could lose ten pounds in two weeks.

That's what we were all going through back then, scared we were gonna have to go to Vietnam.

Did Tony ever talk to you about his dad, Herb?

Not a lot. I never met Herb or his mother. I knew all the brothers. Tony told me once that they had these bunk beds and Tony fell out of the top bunk bed when he was nine or ten. It broke his nose.

That's why Tony's nose was always kind of crooked, because Herb didn't think he needed to take him in to get his nose set. That was the story I heard. Larry corroborated that one; he was in the bottom bunk.

What was Tony driving when you knew him?

When we were still playing together my first car was a 1966 Rambler station wagon. We named it the "Baja Buggy." I sold it to Tony with the understanding you must put a quart of STP in it every fill up, and do not drive this car over 55. Don't Do It.

Well, Tony with his lead foot …

We'd get done playing on Saturday nights in Louisville, and it's only an hour and a half drive to Lexington. So Tony would drive to Lexington every Saturday night so he could visit with Larry, and hang with Larry on Sunday.

Generally, J.D. had an extra gig on Monday nights, with J.D., Larry Rice, Doyle Lawson on guitar, and Bobby Slone. So at any rate, at one of those fill ups, he didn't put the STP in like he should have, so he blew up the Baja Buggy on Newtown Pike, somewhere near New Circle Road. Tony took the plates off it and left it there.

Tony and his cars. That was always a funny thing to me. When

I got out to Lexington, when he was playing with J.D. Crowe, he drove this big, black Chrysler LeBaron. He was heavily enamored with the LeBarons, they were a limited edition. He loved it. I'd ride around Lexington with him. Then when he got out to California you might remember he had a ... I can't remember if it was a Dodge Charger?* ... it was more of a sporty kind of Dodge, and out on the hood there was a Dymo label that said "Spacegrass." That was his car's name, "Spacegrass."

Were you at the Red Slipper the night Clarence White showed up and played?

I wasn't there for that one. I heard about it. Back then, and this was before he got Clarence's guitar, Tony had this guitar that our friend Harry Sparks named "The Wildebeest."

He had Clarence's guitar by the time he moved to California. I mean, Tony could pull good tone out of any guitar.

As a matter of fact, I think a lot of people still don't believe me when I tell them that on the tune "Manzanita," on his *Manzanita* album, Tony played an Ovation guitar on that cut. He did it because he could get more sustain and do these certain slides within the melody that his ol' Martin just ... the note didn't sustain as long.

Ovation gave him this guitar, I guess it was a Glenn Campbell Model Ovation. In his hands, it sounded great. I don't think a lot of people believe me when I tell them, "Nope, he definitely played the Ovation on 'Manzanita.'" The rest of the album is his D-28.

Circling back to Spacegrass, I understand you know the story of how Tony tried to do himself in.

I only heard about that, in that he did the ol' car-in-the-garage-with-the-motor-running. ... I think Leela found him.† I heard

---

* Ron Rice claims it was a white Chrysler Imperial, not a black Le Baron, and that it was actually a '70 Dodge Challenger that wound up as a flood victim in the 1993 "Storm of the Century."
† This story adds that Leela called Bill Wolf who taxied over from San Francisco to their home in Corte Madera. Another story says Bill Wolf found Tony.

about that after the fact.

I was pissed. It was hard to watch Tony go through times when he felt like he was the most shit-on man in music when in fact he had everything going for him.

Sometimes you can't see that. I think he was prone to some depression even back then. Obviously. I was upset with him to the point that when I talked to him, I could say, "What in the hell is wrong with you? How can I help?"

What did he say to that, Sam?

He did admit he had done that. He was in a black hole he couldn't get out of for a little while. But, I'm glad he did. He went on to more excellent things.

What's your understanding of how he died?

He did go into heart failure, but was stuck in the same position while he was still alive, for maybe a day. It's not from an official doctor or from Pam or anyone. I'm not really sure, but that's what I've heard from a person who was able to find out.

Were you there when someone threatened Tony's life?

No, I wasn't there, but in the summer of 1975, the Newgrass Revival played at this famous place in Lexington, the Narcotic Farm, that everyone called the Narc Farm. It had been a place where they sent people who had criminal convictions with narcotics but who also were addicted. For instance, the Narc Farm is where they sent Lenny Bruce at one point.

There was this festival at the old Narcotics Farm grounds. It was a good place to have a festival. And we, the Newgrass Revival, were on it, and I can't remember who else, but I remember J.D. Crowe *&* The New South were on it. He might not have even been calling it "The New South" yet, but J.D., Bobby, Larry and Tony were on the bill. They came to the gig, and Tony never got out of the van except to walk out on stage and play, and then he went immediately back in the van.

He didn't want any of us coming in the van. At first, I remember me and Courtney Johnson going, "What kind of a prima donna has Tony become?" That wasn't it at all.

Apparently he had been threatened by someone and he was only going to get out of that van to go to the stage and back.* Let's say he was concerned that day for his wellbeing. So I wasn't there the night the threat was made, but we saw the amount that he seemed to be freaked out over it at this festival at the Narcotic Farm. I think that was the summer of 1975.

I guess the tour of Japan was his last job with J.D. I didn't realize that at the time. But when he came home from Japan, he stayed in California. Jerry Douglas has a great story Bobby Slone told him:

Tony was rooming with Bobby and they're in Japan. It was September and the room was really hot. The heat system was working in overdrive.

Bobby said Tony picks up the phone, he calls the front desk, and he says, as you know how he would do, "This is Tony Rice from the United States of America. ... ROOM HOT."

And the man at the front desk says, "OPEN WINDOW."

[*We chortle gleefully.*]

Their last show is out on CD now and it's just awesomely great, even though Ricky is ten times louder than J.D.'s banjo ever is.

Last gig you played with him?

IBMA. September 2013. That was the year Tony had come out to be inducted into the Hall of Fame. The guys who played on *Manzanita* were to play with him on the awards show. So Tony shows up and says he doesn't think he can do it; we should get Wyatt.

---

* We'll read about this threat made to Tony's life in Jerry Douglas's interview.

We, meaning the ones who played on *Manzanita:* Tony, Ricky, Jerry, Todd and me. We also had Wyatt as an extra guitarist. So Tony came out, and he had made his speech, which a lot of people enjoyed hearing. Then I had to sing lead, cause Tony couldn't sing lead anymore. And me and Ricky had to switch instruments. Even though Ricky originally played fiddle on "Old Train," and I played mandolin, we needed to switch instruments. He needed to play mandolin and I had to play fiddle, because Ricky was recovering from surgery on his right shoulder. He couldn't play fiddle.[14]

We were an all different version, and then all of a sudden, Tony decided he would play, though he didn't play lead on it. Wyatt did the guitar kickoff.

We played the next night at the IBMA outdoor concert, at the Red Hat Amphitheater. I think it was supposed to be Jerry Douglas, Del McCoury, Alison Krauss, Tony, Mark Schatz and me. We kept wondering: Is he going to make the gig? If he is going to make the gig, are his hands going to work? They were bothering him.

Now, this is mine and his relationship:

He came into the trailer where we were warming up. He played one tune and put his guitar back in the case, and said, "Oh, I'm not warmed up."

To which I said, "Well, how are you going to get warmed up with that thing in the case? Come on, we need to play some."

In fact, he did pretty well that night, though he hadn't been playing. And I know, because I'm only a year younger than him, that if you don't use it, you'll lose it. So, he was rusty but he still played pretty well. That was the last I played with him.

I don't know if he played with anyone after that. And if I'm understanding correctly, that was the last time him and Wyatt played together. It would be a rough thing to do. I'm trusting his instincts that he'd rather not play it than to not feel satisfied doing it. I understand that theory. At my age, I don't always walk off pleased with what I've done. I enjoy playing it and going through the process. I think Tony reached the point he could not enjoy it, and was not happy with the status of what was going on. And he'd already not been singing for years …

May we all know when it's time to stop.

Amen, Brother.

I want to keep playing, but I hope I have the good sense when my hands aren't working anymore to stop doing it in front of people.

Was he a happy guy?

He was when we were around each other. And again, I won't pretend we were around each other the last twenty years of his life. We talked once a year. We stayed in touch.

We loved each other. We told each other we loved each other. So I felt like I could call on him for anything, and I think he felt that way too.

Each person has a different story to tell about Tony, a different angle on a different snapshot.

Mine was coming from [when we were kids]. And I think that still played into how we dealt with each other. We were such kids. The year we were in the band, we got into some of the stupidest arguments.

The Merlefest videos show a Tony who talks little between tunes.

He didn't care if he talked or not. I think that especially after he'd been to California and had become an incredible Miles Davis devotee. He liked it if his talking voice sounded like Miles, and he said he wanted to be like Miles: he didn't want to say thing to the audience.[*]

He spent a lot of time listening to George Benson and Wes

---

[*] Miles Davis's voice became gravely after an operation he had in 1955 to remove a non-cancerous polyp on his larynx. He spoke little on stage, as did Tony.

Montgomery. I wasn't aware of how great George Benson was until Tony made me aware of it. I wouldn't call Tony a jazz guitarist. In some ways he was the ultimate bluegrass guitar player. It fell out of him. It was just natural to him.

I think of him as one of the most progressive guitar players that's ever lived. That being said, I think it's pretty easy to say Tony was one of the most influential guitar players of the last fifty years, if not the most influential acoustic guitarist.

Let's back up a second. A lot of Tony's voicings and things that people associate with Tony, I was there when he was learning them off James Taylor records. He learned an awful lot of chordal and moving lines and things. He loved James Taylor. Tony was the only guy I knew who could play that stuff.

When he joined Bluegrass Alliance, Dan Crary had been doing these fiddle tunes that were exactly the same notes as the fiddle played. And Tony never tried to do that. I don't think it was because he couldn't. He wasn't interested. He didn't care if he played the fiddle tune exactly like it went; he did his own version. And a lot of his versions of those tunes set the standard for how you play them on guitar.

Tony's the guy who named my mandolin "Hoss" after I'd had it a couple of years. Tony believed, and he said it more than once, that his guitar and my mandolin were meant to be played together. And I said, "Yeah, when we're the ones holding them."

I never heard Tony call his guitar any name. Someone was asking me after Tony passed away, "What did he call his guitar?"

I said, "I don't know. You'd have to ask someone else. I'm not sure he called it anything."

I've heard a lot more that it must have been in recent years, when I wasn't around him as much, that he called it "The Antique."

Did Tony ever gave you a nickname?

Not that I'm aware of. You know he had one. He had a nickname for everybody. So he probably had one for me. I don't know.

He used to have the funniest imitation. Apparently I was still kinda shy – I obviously got over that – when we were first playing in the Bluegrass Alliance, and Tony would have a great imitation of me ordering in the restaurant. He would imitate me talking in a normal voice, and then his imitation of me when I ordered from the waitress … you couldn't hear a word I said.

Tony used a lot of language licks, a sentence or a phrase that he'd repeat over and over. Is that right?

Oh yeah. He and I would have a phrase when you know you got the tune right.

He'd go, "You got the lick?"

"Yup, I got the lick."

He'd go, "Great, we got the lick. Let's go."

Or, "How much?"

"Two dollars."

"I'll take it."

He'd get on a riff and stay on it … but I guess I can too, especially when he and I would get together. I don't know which one of us started certain things. We'd just do it together.

Do you remember the last time you spoke with him?

We spoke on the phone probably a couple of years before he died, on September 4. I think I called him that particular time.

I think he actually preferred sometimes for me not to be here and he could leave a nice message for me. We always tried to talk on that date, which is easy for me to remember cause it was my mother's birthday.

He got where he didn't answer the phone and only texted. He

texted in capital letters, all the time. After a while he wouldn't come out of the house, he wouldn't even see anyone.

Jerry and I would often wonder if we should go over and make him come out of the house, but we never got that together. He wouldn't even see his brothers after a while.

Yes. That's the way I understand it. Thank you for your help, Sam. We all miss him very much.

Yup. We do. Poor little feller. We knew he was very fragile. He was more fragile than we all realized.

Bluegrass Alliance – Sam Bush, Courtney Johnson, Tony
Sometime in the early 1970s
Cinematographer unknown

*J*erry Douglas plays a rare instrument, dobro, and plays it masterfully on over 1,600 albums, many with world-renowned musicians,[15] garnering him fourteen Grammies. Jerry fronts his own band, The Jerry Douglas Band, as well as The Earls of Leicester, a group that pays homage to seminal bluegrass band Flatt & Scruggs. He's played with J.D. Crowe & the New South, The Country Gentlemen, Strength In Numbers, and Alison Krauss & Union Station. He had a role in the film, "O Brother, Where Art Thou?"

Jerry knew Tony from 1974 and their time with J.D. Crowe, about four years after Sam Bush and Tony initially hung out. Jerry, like Sam, played Tony's last gig with him at his IBMA Hall of Fame induction, in 2013. (We'll see a photo by Todd Gunsher of Tony and Jerry playing that gig a few pages on.)

I called Jerry on July 12, 2022. He spoke insightfully about issues no one else had mentioned, about what it's like being at the top and the pressures that put on Tony and all who live there.

His description of playing music with Tony put me there as I listened to him gush: "It was like being surrounded by guitars."

Yes, it was.

Jerry Douglas with Vassar Clements

Jerry Douglas Speaks

Jerry, tell me about the Tony Rice you knew.

Or the guy we didn't know. The guy we thought we knew. Tony was a difficult personality all his life, right up to the very end.

I came onto the scene in 1974. I guess that's when all of us met for the first time, Ricky, Tony and I. The first time I met him was at a festival we were all playing. I was there with the Country Gentlemen, and Tony was there with J.D. With Bobby Slone [bass], and Larry Rice [mandolin], we played in Morrow, Ohio, [at the Todd's Fork Outdoor Bluegrass *&* Flea Festival]. It was late October, [starting] to snow. It was really cold. … No one could play the way they wanted to play because of the weather.

The next time I played with him was in the studio on his *California Autumn* record. That just started the ball rolling.

Ricky went with J.D. Crowe *&* The New South. He and Tony both pulled hard to get me on the record, to talk J.D. into letting me play on the record on a couple of tunes.

I guess J.D. relented. He didn't really know know anything about me, but he liked what he heard while we were recording, so I ended up being on eight or nine of the songs instead of two.[16] Then I quit the Country Gentlemen and moved down to Lexington and joined J.D. Crowe *&* The New South.

That was my first solid move. It felt like an upgrade. I was moving into a situation where I was going to learn more music and be a better musician because I was going to be playing with Tony Rice and J.D. Crowe, and I'd always loved J.D.'s playing.

That move was going to improve me as a musician just by learning, from osmosis, from soaking up whatever they were doing. I ended up playing with them at the Holiday Inn a couple of times. Then it all moved out to the Sheraton a little north of town, a new hotel. I don't know what J.D. was thinking about, whether this was a better gig or not after being at the Holiday Inn for all of those years.

I moved into the same apartment complex that Tony and Ricky lived in. I had just gotten married and took a one-bedroom there at Larkin Terrace Apartments. We later joked on Boone Creek's records about naming things like the Larkin Terrace string section, the Larkin Terrace singers … all kinds of stuff.

Tony was a really a funny guy. He was always cracking jokes and laughing. He had a great laugh. He was really great to be around.

I remember one time, Tony and I played Berryville, Virginia at the bluegrass festival there.* Later on that first night, Tony and I took that fancy van and went driving thru the fields looking for pot. We wanted to smoke a joint. We weren't carrying anything ourselves. We just went out in the fields, and we had fog lights on this van. And I said, "Tony, hit the fog lights."

He hit the lights and we bounced up over this field. They grew watermelons on this field all year long, and then they had this festival. So we're driving through there, and I see people diving to save their sight from these fog lights we had going on, they were so bright and it was putting people's eyes out everywhere. People were diving under mattresses into the tents to get away from us while Tony and I were laughing like crazy people.

---

* In 1974, the Berryville Bluegrass Festival appears to have taken place around July 15.

We didn't get any marijuana; we just went back to the hotel and laughed all the way there. That was one of the funniest nights I ever spent with Tony Rice. Just me and him out there, both just acting like a couple of teenagers, being fools. It was so much fun. I got so much out of it. I'll never forget it. It was Tony being Tony.

It was the closest I got to me and Tony just being us.

We were always close, and always loved seeing each other, it was always a big hug. But you got that from Tony no matter what. Tony was a hugger. Tony would see you and he'd come with his arms stretched out as far as they would go. He was just a lover guy. He loved his friends, he loved being with them.

I would wait till Tony woke up, which was like four or five in the afternoon, go over and hang with him and his then-wife, Kate.

Tony had a fish tank in his house then, and most his life, I think. He never had more than one or two fish, but he'd name them. He had a black molly, a little black fish with bulging eyes. He named it Santo. He had one of those Dymo labelers. He put one on the aquarium and it said, "Now Shit, Santo." That's all it said.

[*Large laughter*]

I was 19 years old and I was still trying to figure out everything. I remember the oddest things. And that was one of them. He'd sit and have conversations with Santo.

[*He laughs heartily.*]

And, he'd talk to the fish.* I would talk to the fish. We'd both yell at the fish.†

The fish wouldn't do anything we asked them to. It was funny because of that. It wasn't a dog; it was a fish. It was like having a dog that couldn't hear or didn't give a shit.

I went to Japan with the New South in 1975. So I was only in the New South from June until we came back from Japan in

---

* Uh-oh.
† Double Uh-oh.

September. Tony had decided he was moving to San Francisco to play with David Grisman. I've heard several people float different theories as to why he did that.

I understood that as a musical move, and aren't we all glad he did it. I think it was a hard thing for him to do, to move from Lexington and from J.D., whom he did love. He and Crowe were really good friends, and they were the leaders of that band.

Ricky got there and … he was very ambitious. He had many things he tried to insert into it. But from what I could see when I got there, it was J.D. and Tony steering the boat.

I would wait until Tony woke up and go hang with him. He would get up at 5 o'clock in the evening and have something to eat. Sooner or later we'd all end up going to the club. As soon as we got back that night, Kate would make breakfast and we'd just eat bacon and eggs and toast and all kinds of stuff at Tony's house and then I'd wander on home and Ricky would wander on home and that was the end of the day.

What was the other reason Tee might have quit J.D. to go with Grisman?

The other reason was something that I witnessed.

The first festival show I did with them was "The Festival of the Bluegrass," in Lexington. So we're getting ready to play, and all of a sudden there's a commotion and I … What's going on?

We had a camper for a dressing room trailer and this guy comes up and says that Tony had impregnated his sister, and he was going to shoot Tony that day on stage.

And we were all like, "Oh, great."

The only thing Bobby Slone said was, "Don't stand next to Tony during the show."

There's this theory that has floated around that Tony got the hell out of Lexington because of that and went west. I don't know how true that is.

I know what happened that day. The guy threatened Tony. It visibly affected him. The guy threatened his life and then left.

That was [the other] theory.

Everyone said that Tony left at the end of the summer. He was getting out of Lexington if this guy was looking for him. Tony had a problem with fidelity ... [*he laughs*] ... with infidelity.

Pressure, Anxiety & Mental Problems

Tony liked being married. He liked having someone. He had Kate and then he had Leela. We all loved Leela. I couldn't figure out what happened with Leela, but I have an idea.

Tony was starting to have some problems, some mental problems, stuff we all have. He was the best guitar player in this genre of music. He felt that pressure even though it's not something that should drive us nuts and make us do funny things.

We're musicians, and some of us are better musicians than others, and just have this innate ... He was just gifted. He had a gift. And he used it playing and singing. From the time he was a tiny kid, he wanted to be that, and now he was that, and he was the best. And people were following him around and telling him how great he was all the time. That can get to you.

And I think with Leela, it was his mental incapacity to deal with it [that] was starting to present. He was starting to be depressed, have love anxiety. But I imagine that was with him most of his life.

I suffer from it too, and I don't know of a great musician who doesn't suffer from anxiety to some degree once you get to a certain plateau. If you don't deliver what's expected of you, it's a "What's wrong with him?" situation.

Tony was starting to suffer from that and from making records and trying to make each record mean something. There was a lot of self-imposed pressure. We all do that.

I think that Leela must have got tired of it, couldn't deal with it and couldn't solve it. He wasn't really seeing anybody to help him with it. He was dumping it all on her. I don't know of any things that happened to them, any infidelities or anything like that, but that was in Tony.

We all thought that Leela was the best thing that ever happened to Tony. At that point Tony showed us all that he sometimes had problems with just being able to deal with day-to-day. I understand that now. I didn't totally understand it then, but I knew that the guy was in pain of some kind.

I never blamed him when he would come into the studio, and he just couldn't do it. We'd all be there and we'd spend a whole day waiting for him to get there. It was like the Elvis syndrome of having a studio full of people ready to play, but not knowing what they were going to play. Then you show up and you can't emotionally get through it.

We'd try something, and Tony would go, "Man, I can't do it."

I remember one time being in the studio with J.D. Crowe, Vassar Clements, and Sam Bush ... and we didn't do anything. We spent all day waiting. Then Tony got there and we couldn't do anything. And there was more than one day like that.

I've seen other artists do that too. It's usually coming from an emotional drain, and too much going on where you can't do your job. Unfortunately, we were all sitting there and the money wheel was spinning, but we were not getting anything done.

That was really a dark period. That was the darkest of the recording times that I remember. It was bad.

Leela was helping him guide his life, his musical life and his personal life, trying to keep his feet on the ground. It's not an easy thing to do. In Tony's case, he had all this hero worship going on all around him, but at home he was just this normal guy, who he really wanted to be.

As you'll remember, he took up photography. Anything he took up, it was like OCD.* He'd get into it. He'd read everything he could read about it. It became watch repair later on in life. That was what he did; he didn't do anything but that. He wasn't even interested in playing the guitar anymore.

It hurt. It hurt to play the guitar.

I think there was a lot of pain in his arthritic joints and his thumb, and his wrists. I imagine there were some carpal problems and trigger fingers, ... I don't know what. He had problems with his ulnar[17] from overuse. A lot of it happens because things just wear out. And we have to get them repaired. There are ways to repair them.

Paul Simon talks to Jerry about Tony

I opened for Paul Simon one summer. I was really worried about Tony at this point. This was 2006, I think. Paul and I got to be close and talked about things. I brought up Tony, and all these things that were wrong, with his voice, with his hands, with his dysphonia [also known as hoarseness].

I was standing in a catering line, waiting in line with a plate in my hand, but I didn't get to any food, because I had said something to Paul.

He walked up to me and said, "Ya know, your friend, all those things can be repaired and he can go on."

We stood there for 45 minutes talking about that, and finally somebody saw we weren't going anywhere, we weren't going to do anything, so somebody got us food, and we sat down and talked about it.

He said, "This dysphonia, that can be repaired."'

Julie Andrews had just lost her voice by a botched surgery. And

---

* Obsessive-compulsive disorder is a pattern of unwanted thoughts and fears (obsessions) that lead you to do repetitive behaviors (compulsions). These obsessions and compulsions can cause distress. That's Wikipedia talking.

for Julie Andrews to lose her voice on Broadway was just like somebody died. But that had been repaired. She was back, she was singing better than ever.

He said "Any of these things can be repaired, if you want to get them fixed."

I thought, *I don't think Tony wants to get it fixed. I don't think Tony wanted to be him any more.*

I've gotten to that point where I don't want to be me all the time either. When you've been doing this for fifty years, you think, There's gotta be more to life than this.

I think Tony's injuries and singing too much and smoking and drinking and alcohol dried out his throat. Tony was singing too high for the register of his natural voice. He stretched it out, and he made all those things happen.

He was responsible for the things that eventually made him stop playing. That was all self-induced, not on purpose, but he was drinking an awful lot for a long time before he finally stopped and wised up. He could quote you the Big Blue Book from A.A. [Alcoholics Anonymous] from cover to cover.

But whether he was living it or not, I don't know.

He had a problem with pills, not with uppers, not speed or anything like that. Just pain. I think that even in his best days he was taking things to get him through the pain of playing, and that exacerbated the problem. He got addicted to some things that didn't help him later on. He was not fixing anything; he was making it worse.

John Starling[*] told him, "I can fix this; I can fix your voice if you'll let me."

But he wouldn't let him.

It was a sad thing playing out in front of us. We did benefit after benefit. When Tony would get in trouble, we'd try to get him out of it, help him out. But he would repeat it again.

---

[*] Starling was a musician and an otolaryngological physician.

Until he got in A.A., he was wrecking cars and waking up in waist-deep water because he'd run off the road into a river. Things like that. He finally stopped that.

He quit drinking and that seemed to calm things down a lot, but there was still this dysphonia, that he couldn't sing. When you're a great singer and all of a sudden your voice is taken away from you, you're going to go deeper into your depression, your anxiety is going to increase. It's something God gave you and then you took it away. God did not take it away. Tony did the damage himself, all by himself.

We all tried to help, we tried to help him mentally, by telling him, "Look dude, this is going to be all right. You're you; we're us. We're here to help you, we'll stand behind you, we'll do whatever it takes to get you through this show," and then he would immediately retreat somewhere.

It's a sad character, but he kind of wanted that too, in a way, because he worshiped Miles Davis, John Coltrane, and Eric Dolphy. Any time you went to his house, he would put on something. He listened to nothing but straight-up jazz. I don't know why he was still interested in playing bluegrass at all, except that it was a part of his DNA.

He'd gone to school on Miles Davis and all of these great jazz guys, and he wanted to live the life of a jazz guy. He didn't shoot heroin, but I think he thought about it.

I think he thought about going the whole route. He dressed like them and he lived like them, up to a point. I don't think he got into anything like that. People used to tell me, "He must do a lot of cocaine, because of the way he breathes and the way he sings."

No, I've never seen Tony Rice even come close to cocaine. Never. His thing was drinking and smoking, and that was it.

The jazz guys that he wanted to emulate included Miles. He said, "Miles Davis took a sabbatical."

And I said, "Yeah but Miles Davis had tons of money in the bank when he did it, when he took a sabbatical; he didn't just quit for two years. He lived his normal life, but he took a sabbatical to get away for a little while, to reacquaint himself with it, I guess." But Tony liked living that life.

He had different things he would go into, the John Wilkes Booth thing, which I didn't understand, never understood. But Tony had a real fascination for John Wilkes Booth, down to the point where I think he owned one of Booth's jackets, one of his coats. And he had a copy of it made and he wore it on his *Native American* album cover.

There's even a song on *Native American* about John Wilkes Booth that Mary Chapin Carpenter wrote.[18] I remember Chapin coming into the studio with the finished version of it because Tony asked her to rewrite something. She came in and we cut the song.

And I thought, *This is odd. This is a new level for Tony.*

I never really got into politics with him, but he was wearing Rush Limbaugh ties. That big yellow tie that's in all these pictures, that's a Rush Limbaugh tie.

I think he liked listening to that stuff, but he didn't talk about politics in front of me. I didn't hear it. I knew that he was of that ilk, but I never talked with him about politics at all. I don't know how I got out of that, but I did.

I didn't hear any rants. Did you? Did you witness any of that?

No, but when I saw John Wilkes Booth books lying around the house, I thought, Who would be a student of Booth except someone who thought he did a good thing in murdering Lincoln?

Yes. I've got to wonder if Tony was more interested in the

SOLD

Rush's Personal Necktie - Triangle Blue

$500.00

This personal tie of Rush Limbaugh's was apparently sold to Tony.
– photographer unknown

lifestyle of Booth and the way he always dressed better than the other actors. Tony may have seen some parallels in their lives and latched onto him. I don't know whether he would have been a fan of killing Lincoln. Maybe Tony thought Lincoln was evil and that he did the wrong things. But his fascination with Booth was a crazy thing. I don't understand it, and I don't know when it happened.

I was busy doing other things. I wasn't always attached to him, but when he wanted to do something special or make a record, that's when he would call. Or play in the band, or sit in with the band when we were at the same festival. I would do that automatically, because I loved Tony. I loved the way he played, what he thought. I felt sorry for him too because I knew he was tortured.

Once we got finished playing, Tony and I didn't talk. We talked when we played. We had a lot in common at that point. When that stopped, the commonness stopped as well.

The last time I played with Tony was when he spoke to the IBMA at his induction into the Hall of Fame, in September, 2013.

He got in touch with his higher power[*] and this voice came out that I'd been hearing all along from him. He could speak like that at any point as long as he didn't get above a certain decibel; he could sound like Tony Rice 1975. But he couldn't sing that way and he couldn't speak beyond a certain level, or we would go into that guttural [zone] and his voice would close down.

But that night he stood out there telling those people that some day he thought he could sing and always would, kind of thing. I went "Whoa Tony. You're making these people believe in the second coming or something, and this isn't right." We were standing backstage, because we were ready and lined up to kick off "Old Train."

I had Wyatt there because Tony hadn't played in two or three years, I had Wyatt come to kick the tune off and play rhythm guitar because I didn't think Tony would be involved in it at all, though we did leave a microphone open at the other end of the line. So it was Wyatt, me, Ricky, Sam, and probably Todd Phillips.

I said to Ricky, when I heard him out there talking and what he was saying, and I said, "Ricky, knowing what we know, what do we do about this?"

---

[*] I think Tony said, "My heavenly Father"

And Ricky said, "Nothing, nothing."

And so that was it: Nothing.

And just to be clear, what do you mean by "this"?

"This" was Tony talking to a hall full of people in a voice that he was conjuring up through his higher power. OK, there is a higher power, I believe that, but I started hearing something that I've been hearing all along from him, which was this voice. As long as he didn't speak and push his voice beyond a certain decibel, he could sound like that … forever, from whenever this throat stuff started happening he could still do that. And he was telling these people it was a special occasion that he could do this. And I thought that was not fair to these people, it wasn't true.

I heard people screaming "Hallelujah" and all this stuff, and I was like, *This is P.T. Barnum stuff right here.*

You can speak. This is not a special occasion. Your higher power of course gave you this voice, but did not present this moment for you to showcase all the work you've been doing. This is pissing me off. It's not right to make people think that you're going to sing and do all these things right now.

Wyatt was talking to me, he was saying, "He's going to come up here and he's going to kick the song off."

I said, "No he's not, Wyatt; you're going to kick the song off. That's the reason you're here. You sound the most like him that anybody ever will. And because we don't know if he can play or not, you're going to kick the song off, because you're going sound like Tony Rice 1980 or whenever we did this."

So Wyatt kicked the song off, and Tony put that guitar on, and he hit that open mic, and as soon as I heard his guitar, I went, "Oh, man. He sounds great. That's Tony. Nobody else makes that sound but Tony."

I imagine Wyatt was shaking in his boots, but Tony didn't try to take it over. He let Wyatt kick it off. We stood there in disbelief that Tony was even doing this after not playing for however long.

Bleeding on the Strings with the Usual Suspects

I knew that Tony would come back next night, because there was this big check involved, and he was supposed to play in this big thing with Sam and I, the usual suspects. Tony got up to play all these songs, and he played well.

By the end of the next night, Tony's hands were bleeding because he hadn't played, he didn't have any callouses. But he was being Tony Rice without rehearsal, without playing. It was all muscle memory. Everything he did was muscle memory, and some of it failed, but it was Tony.

The night after the awards, where he gave the speech, he drove back home to Reidsville. Then he drove back to Raleigh the next day. He didn't stay in Raleigh. He drove home and then he came back.* He called me about an hour before the show and said "How do I get there?"

I said, "Tony, I don't live in Raleigh, I can't tell you how to get here. I don't have a GPS; I don't know where you are. Call Nancy Cardwell," who was the president of the IBMA at that point.

It was painful to watch because we all know what it feels like to play guitar on those little wires when you have no callouses. When you're just starting to play, you kinda know what to do, but if you don't play guitar all the time, like I don't …. If I play guitar for a set, I'm in pain for two days.

I imagine that was happening with Tony because his left-hand fingers were bleeding from pulling-off, hammering, all the things that Tony Rice does. It was strange, strange to say the least. And as soon as he was done, he was out of there.

That was the last time I saw Tony.

---

* This is a distance of 95 miles, roughly an hour and a half drive each way.

I know if I had gone to his house, he wouldn't have let me in. He didn't let his brothers in; he didn't let his uncle Frank Poindexter in. He would come out and sit in their car for a short time and then he would go back into the house. His anxiety had reached such a level that he couldn't even deal with his family. He couldn't talk; he couldn't speak to them.

He'd gone on to some other plane at that point. I know about mental illness but not to the point where Tony was. He had to be a lonely, lonely guy at that point.

He had Pam and India,* but no one else. He didn't let anybody else in the house. Pam had some heart problems and she moved into an apartment complex.

But Tony did call me; he called me out of the blue one afternoon. He said, "Ya know, Pam takes this heart medicine and sometimes she talks crazy, like out of her head. But she said something to me the other day that made sense."

She said, "Your friends probably all hate you, because you never talk to them, you don't converse, you don't tell them anything. It's like you just left them."

And he said, "That hurt my feelings, and I understood that and so I'm calling you guys to let you know."

It was like a text from him. He was talking other-wordly, like, "I love you guys. I never wanted it to get this way. I never wanted to leave you guys wondering about me."

He said, "She's right. I should stay in contact. You guys are my friends. I love you and I'm not trying to avoid you. My depression and my anxiety … I can barely leave the house."

That one last call that I got from him. He didn't call Sam about this same thing. And he didn't call nobody else that I know of; nobody's spoken of it. I just out of the blue had that conversation with him about Pam telling him that his good friends probably

---

* India, a.k.a. Dawn (her middle name), is Pamela's daughter.

were mad at him because he never talked to them anymore. And this was his way of trying to patch it up a little bit, just let me know that he loved me and all the cool things we'd done together.

We talked and laughed for a solid hour. And then, that was it. That was it.

IT.

I never talked to him again.

Was he saying goodbye to you?

I don't think so. I think he was trying to explain his illness. At that point, he couldn't even leave the house; he didn't want to leave the house. His anxiety was so bad that he couldn't face anybody.

He couldn't leave the house is the truth. He had someone delivering groceries to him so he wouldn't have to go out. There had been a Gofundme* page set up for him at that point. But when he died, they found so many uncashed checks in his desk and all over the house, just checks everywhere that people had written to him, and he'd never cashed them, even gig checks. He'd just forgot about them.

My friend, a lawyer, is taking care of the estate. He's gotten all of us out of trouble in North Carolina at some point. He's a really good lawyer and a bluegrass fan, and as huge a fan of Tony Rice as anybody.

I thought, "Buddy, please get involved in this, because Pam can't do this, India can't do this. They need help."

He volunteered and they took him in. He made sure the guitar was OK, that it was intact. No strings have been played. Pam won't let the guitar go. It's locked up in a good vault; it's safe.

But there's no telling what's going to happen to that guitar. I don't think anything will happen with that guitar as long as Pam is with us. The guitar is okay.

---

* Gofundme is a U.S. crowd-funding platform.

When they cleaned the house, they took away a ton of dog shit.* Tony had not kept up the place. The only place in the house that was safe to walk in was where he did his watch repairs. The house had to be completely stripped of all surfaces. He had a bunch of standard poodles in there. Their output is strong, let's say. The house was a mess. We can say that. When they came in to take care of the house, it was not any place that anyone would want to live in.

When he went away, when he snailed back into that shell, for all intents and purposes he died to us then. He went away. It was like Tony died but he was still walking around. It was very odd for us. Wanting to play with him but knowing he wasn't going to do it.

This record that we cut with Béla was *Tales from the Acoustic Planet*. It was right after *Drive* [released 1988]. Tony played on it, we all played on it, we were going to do a tour of it, and all of a sudden Tony said, "I was throwing a cup of coffee out the convertible window and I hit my left hand on the wing of the window, and now I can't play."

He essentially canceled his part of the tour at that point, and we went, "Oh God, what do we do?" That's when Bryan Sutton came and saved the tour for us by subbing for Tony.

That was the first time Tony dropped us, or didn't know why he did it. I didn't really believe the "I'm incapacitated because I threw a cup of coffee out the window" story. Maybe he did it, but that wasn't what was keeping him from doing the tour.

I think what was keeping him from doing the tour was he didn't like it if he couldn't drive his car. He was becoming a hermit at that point, making it more difficult to get him from festival to festival, and things like that.

Something was wrong. Something was totally way off. It was like a car wreck you're watching and you can't take your eyes off of

---

* The Medical Examiner's Report notes the "immense amounts of animal feces throughout the house."

it. We knew something was going on with Tony. We didn't know what it was, but we couldn't stop wondering. It came up a lot.

What are we going to do? How can we help Tony?

There wasn't a way anymore. I gave up except for trying to call him on his birthday, trying to call him out of the blue.

Bryan Sutton said, "The only way I've been able to get an answer from Tony is to text him." So I texted him. I was in Montreal, at the Montreal Jazz festival, and I texted Tony and he texted back immediately.

He said, all in caps, all the time ... it's like his phone was stuck on caps. I think it was because he had a flip phone, and he didn't want to go between the little letters and the big ones, so he stayed in caps. He said to me,

I DON'T DO VOICE MAIL. I DON'T DO EMAIL. I DO THIS NEW KIND OF MAIL CALLED TEX.

["Tex" ... *we laugh.*]

So we kept going: What I was texting him about was coming down to play on a thing I wanted to do with me, Earl Scruggs and Tony. Just to play "Home Sweet Home" with those two guys.

So we did it a few times. Earl was in great shape. Earl played faster than I actually wanted him to. And Tony took a couple of solos and one of the solos I had to take out. I couldn't use it. It was hard. The second solo I kept.

He drove up from North Carolina to do the set. He was there for two days. I got him a nice hotel here. And at the end of two days he was gone. No nothing, just, "Bye."

I guess it's okay 'cause I got what I needed. I sure would have liked to have my pal around for a minute, just to talk to, but that wasn't going to happen. He just entered this alternate life that didn't have anything to do with us unless we needed him for something, and then he would come.

But I don't think he was playing very much. I think he was

making the transfer to watch mechanic.

Alison Krauss & Union Station
We had Tony come play the Grand Ol' Opry with us, with AKUS, Alison Krauss & Union Station. There was a huge response.

And we said, "Why don't we play a tour and we'll do some of our songs. We'll do a whole set of your songs. And you just play guitar. Dan Tyminski will sing or Alison will sing. We'll do the songs in as close as we can do to the keys of the originals. So you can play exactly what you played."

He did that, but he drove his Mustang instead of riding the bus. And some of these things were over 500 miles a night. It worked out pretty good for the first four or five, and then Tony started missing sound checks because he had to drive all night long.

He had another guy with him to help him drive, but he would not let the other guy take the wheel. So Tony's driving this Mustang with this guitar in the back and he's driving like 90 miles an hour to make the gig. I don't think he got any tickets or anything like that. He showed up at every gig.

But right before the tour started, I took him out to dinner here, and he gave me one of his watches, one of his Spaceviews.

It is one of my more prized possessions of life at this point. And I wear it a lot. And people come up to me and they'll go, Hey look, I've got one too." It's like a Tony Rice thing. If you've got a Spaceview watch, it's because of Tony Rice. It's not because of Accutron.

When I first came into the band, one of the first things I noticed was Tony was wearing this watch. I'd never seen anything like it.

And he said, "This shit went to the moon, dude." In Tony's voice, ya know [in graveled voice]: "Ah, this shit went to the moon."

It was made for the astronauts, really, and then publicized as such. And Tony went crazy, got a Spaceview, and that's all he ever wore. He didn't go in for the other fancier Accutron ones, not really. He maybe did later on, but while I was working with him, he always had that one watch or maybe he had two.

For him to give me that watch before we went on the tour was like handing me the keys to the kingdom. I felt very close and very fortunate at that point.

Tony with Alison Krauss at the wheel of his 1985 Lincoln Town Car
– photograph by Mark Schatz, circa 1988

For dinner that night, Tony ordered surf and turf, "Ahl 'ave surf 'n' turf," a lobster tail and a fillet. I'd never seen him eat so much. I didn't believe he would even eat that much, but he ate the whole damned thing. And it was like watching a starving man eat. He was so hungry. It was all sad, and happy, and thank God, and we're going on this tour, and I said "Hey Tony, there's a window up there on the van, you can push this little button, and you can blow smoke all night long, I'll get you a fake steering wheel, you can drive all you want to …" But he would not ride the bus.

Accutron Spaceview
– photographer unknown

Did Tony every talk about his dad, Herb?

Herb died from a fire, a lit cigarette in a bed. About two weeks later, we went out on a *Bluegrass Album* band tour.* And I remember it was Thanksgiving, and I had to buy my Thanksgiving dinner at a restaurant that day, and I swore I'd never do that again.

But Herb died and then Tony decided to go ahead and do the tour. And I thought, *Whoa. I don't know if I could do something like that.*

But he did, and he was sad, but he was Tony Rice and he did

---

* *Bluegrass Album, Vol. 3 – California Connection*

his job. It was a sad tour, very melancholy, I knew that the guy had just lost his father and he's out here … I guess this is therapy. Where else would he be? You're doing something Dad would love to do.

We didn't talk about it on purpose because we didn't want to throw Tony into a spiral of some kind, and lose him too. But it was really a sad thing, for me.

I kept thinking, *Man, I don't know how he can do this. I don't know how he can keep it together.* But he did and he was just really quiet. He did everything … to the best of his ability.

That's the only time I heard him talk about Herb. I got the idea that his dad was probably as tortured as Tony ever was. He drank. He drank a lot. That's evidently what ended up getting him. He passed out in bed with a cigarette in his hand and died.

We all kind of wondered, Why are we here?

He wants you here because you do what you do and he needs that, and he's your friend. And that's my angle on all of it.

Did you know that Kate passed away a few years ago?

No I didn't. She was really sweet. She was great. And she tried, she tried. Tony wasn't very fair to her. She worked her ass off. I remember taking her to work …

That was another thing we'd do, take Kate to work. And Kate would work until she got off that night, get a ride home, and then when we got home, she'd fix breakfast.

I just thought she was the sweetest; I loved her. I thought she was pretty great and I thought she was forever, but the next time I went to Sir Francis Drake,* she wasn't there.

---

* the street Tony lived on in Corte Madera

Tony's Way with Words

You know how Tony would get a phrase and wear it out? Like …
"I fergit where I am." There was always something that he would
repeat to you at least twenty times a day.

You just laugh. It was funny. It was Tony's way of being funny.
That's what he came up with. He'd say that, and he'd get a great
response and then he could go back to being himself again.

Knowing more about mental illness now, I know that a lot of
these things are camouflage for how someone is feeling. "I'm
gonna say something funny to set this thing back on its ear again,
and off we go. This gets the attention off of me and moves it on to
something else."

It was a reflex. It wasn't him trying to be funny. It was a reflex.
And that's why he'd repeat them. Because he knew they'd get a re-
action from us. We laughed every time. That was what he needed.
That fed him and he could go on.

I wish he'd taken all the advice he got from us and boiled it
down to, "Tony we love you; please get some help." But I don't
know that he ever did.

How can he not have, at some point, as intelligent as he was, go
to somebody and say, "Look, what's wrong with me? This is something I can't figure out. Can you help me?"

It seems it would be unlike Tony not to do that, but I don't know
that he did. That's the Tony Rice I know.

He was a tormented soul as long as I'd known him. He could
laugh like anyone else. But underneath there he was tore up.

There was something there that kept coming back. Maybe it's
something that happened in his childhood … At age 19, he really
thought he had granuloma, and that this was what was going to
kill him. At that early point in his life, he thought something was
going to kill him.

He told me, "Till I was about 11 years old, I thought Larry

Jerry Douglas and Tony at the Red Hat Amphitheater, 9/27/2013, IBMA

– photo by Todd Gunsher

[Tony's brother] was a Mexican." I don't know where we were or why he said that. It was just Tony inserting his weird sense of humor into whatever it was we were doing.

When he said it, it was f'ing hilarious. It was like pandemonium. We all laughed our asses for a while, then we got back to normal.

But it stuck with me. It was funny. It was sad.

If you want to be depressed, you can enjoy wallowing in your depression. I know because I've done it. You can enjoy being the cast out. You can enjoy being whatever you want to invent in your mind. You can enact that situation if you're depressed enough and you're enjoying your depression, you can go on with all the things right up to pulling that trigger ... and then it's too late.

I think Tony could bring those things back to the surface any time he wanted to. And I think that they finally ate him.

I'll say it again: We all were waiting for the day when we'd hear that Tony got help and Tony was on the road to recovery. I had that thought and I wanted that to happen and every time we thought we were getting close, he would fly back. But there was nothing we as friends could do.

Out of our own "fight-or flight," we decided to let Tony go. That's what I did. I let Tony go to the point that I would only get my news about Tony from Frank Poindexter or Wyatt.

Tony's Last Years
I don't know who would have had [face to face] contact with Tony in the last years ... Anybody who tried, he wouldn't let them in the house. He didn't really talk. I've sent countless messages to Tony that went unanswered. Forever.

What's your understanding of what Tony died of?

My understanding is that Tony didn't die on Christmas, that he died a couple days before Christmas, but he was found Christmas.

And what did he die of, do you think?
I don't know. There was lots of Xanax* around. He wasn't drinking.

I think maybe Tony got down to like 90 pounds. And I think his body just quit. I think maybe he had a heart attack. He still smoked a lot.

I don't know, and my friend who is taking care of the estate hasn't told me, out of not wanting me to know. But he did not die of a self-inflicted anything. He died standing beside the stove.

And when I heard Ricky say he was making coffee for breakfast, I thought, *Darn it, Ricky, Tony didn't eat breakfast.* He went to bed at nine or 10 o'clock in the morning, or a little bit earlier. He was up all night. Tony made coffee at night. He didn't make coffee in the morning.

I think he was making coffee at night, whatever night it was, and he had a heart attack. Or some seizure of some kind, and that killed Tony. He was all alone, and he had nobody to come check on him, so he was just there.

What's your understanding of how Pamela and Tony ended up not living together?
Tony told me that Pam had had a heart attack and wanted to move closer into town to be closer to her doctors. Now that's what Tony told me.

Pam and India, they open that guitar case and that's Tony to them, to Pam and to India and to anyone who's left. There is no Tony anywhere. That guitar is Tony.

---

* Xanax is a sedative to treat anxiety and panic disorder. A controlled substance, it can cause paranoid ideation and impair memory and judgment. Combined with other substances, particularly alcohol, it can slow breathing and possibly lead to death.

He put the strings on it, he put the picks up in between the strings on the headstock. And Pam won't let anybody take those out. And I think it's a situation where Pam is going to have that guitar until there is no Pam. It's hers.

I don't know if there is a will. I don't think so. He always told Wyatt he was going to give him that guitar. I don't know how he was actually going to do that.

The guitar is in a safe place right now. I wish Wyatt could play that guitar and it should rightfully be his guitar to play, but it's at least a half million dollar guitar.

Another thing crossed my mind while this was going on with Tony. There are plenty of people out there who have great big billfolds … deep pockets, who would buy that guitar from Tony and let him play it. And he could take that money and he could get out of debt, he could get his throat fixed, he could get his hand fixed.

He could do all of these things that would clear up all of these problems and all these things he would say why he couldn't do, why he couldn't play anymore. They were all solvable things, as Paul Simon told me. That guitar was the way out, but he wouldn't do it. He was resigned to dying the way he died, I'm pretty sure. He didn't want to have anything to do with playing the guitar or singing. He was done.

This is what I think was going through his mind: *How could he be as good – even if he got repaired everywhere – how could he do what he did before, without letting people down, without being an imitation of himself?*

I wonder if that went through his head and he decided "There's no way I can do this, so I'm not going to do it. I can't be that. I'm not that guy." That was the end of it. That was his mindset from there on out. I think if I got all my things repaired and I couldn't play as fast as I could when I was 30 years old, I would wonder if I would want to do that or not. I already did that. Why would I want to do that again?

Aren't we old enough to see there is an arc of life, and we've lived through the crown and now we are at a different point of life?

That's right. That's where I am. And Tony understood that too. Tony was a very intelligent guy. He had to think of that, and think it all the way through. And I think, "Yeah this is where I am in my life. I'm Tony Rice. I can't be that Tony Rice, so I will not be Tony Rice."

Maybe that's it. Maybe that's it.

I look at it as he's submitted to life on his terms. He wasn't going to be that guy anymore, so he wasn't going to pretend. He wasn't going to have operations done so he could attempt to be that. He had been that and he was done.

I have a bass player friend who had a severe arthritic thumb prob-lem. She had an operation to correct it. A couple years later I asked her, "How did it go?" She said, "I wish I hadn't had it done." Which is to say her hand was worse off than it was before.

Yeah I know that can happen.

And I'm sure Paul is talking about, "These are the best doctors in the world." And they don't botch things. If it didn't work they'd fix it. He was so matter of fact when he was telling me that stuff. He was saying there's no need for your friend to go down this way. This can be fixed. This can be repaired.

But I don't think Tony wanted it to be repaired.

And yeah, I understand that about operations. They're not all a success. But if you wanted to go that way, and you had that much inspiration left in you, then you would do it to try to get it better. And if it didn't work, you are right back where you were or ... sue somebody.

I don't think Tony was ever going to go that route, and that conversation I had [with Paul Simon], I never told Tony about it.

Last time I talked to Tony, I decided as soon as I heard his voice on the phone, that I was not going to tell him anything, tell him what to do. I was going to listen to him, tell him I loved him, listen to him. If I didn't agree with him I wouldn't say anything, but if I agreed with him I wouldn't tell him I agreed with him either.

But it wasn't going to be a downer conversation from me, it was going to be as up as I could get it. I decided, all these times we talked to him about doing this, this could make things better or … it might make it better for us, but we weren't him. Everybody's got a different way of taking advice, even from their friends, anybody, about what you should do …

It's like … "Nah. I'm going to do what I'm going to do, and if you've got a great idea, I'll take it, I'll think about it," but, I don't think his mind was made up at that point. He wasn't going to do anything about it. I think he lived those last few years like he wanted to. He worked on watches.

He didn't have to deal with the music. He kept as many people out as he could. He was totally in charge of what was going on with him. I think that Accutrons kept him going as long as he did. I think he had guns. He didn't shoot himself, or anything like that.

I know he had at least one revolver.

Yeah. Probably lots. I don't think he had the infatuation for guns that he had for watches and cameras. Remember when he used to take so many pictures of everything? That was Leela. That's when the photography thing came in. That was Leela who got him interested in photography. And she was such a good photographer.

Tony knew that I was a minister. He asked me to officiate his marriage to Leela. I married them.

You did? Good man.

It was my shortest-lived marriage.

[*Jerry laughs.*]

It wasn't because of you, Bill. We sure know that. When she was done, she was done. She was outta there. The End.

He had demons all the time. She was the one who chased them away until she wasn't there anymore. She got tired of living that way. She was young, beautiful, her whole life ahead of her. She had to make a decision and probably made the right one.

And, oh man, we loved her, we loved her. You must have too.

When somebody's that distant all the time, and I know this from personal behavior. I can get very distant when that stuff starts coming on.

I'm actually doing something about it. I'm deep into some regression therapy* at this point and trying to find out, what the hell, why does this stuff happen? Turning over every rock, trying to figure it out, because I don't like it and I don't want to end up like Tony.

There was one point when Tony put a tube from the exhaust pipe into his car. That was during Leela … I think.

He went into the garage underneath his apartment on Sir Francis Drake Boulevard, and he piped up ol' Spacegrass [Tony's 1970s Dodge Challenger] into his window. She found him before he was passed out. She caught him.†

And no one was more mad than Sam Bush. "You sonofabitch, you do this without saying goodbye?"

I remember those were Sam's words to me. He and Tony had such a past, going all the way back to Louisville, and all that stuff.

But when the exhaust thing happened, it got around to just a few of us. It was Sam who actually told me.

---

* An approach to treatment focusing on resolving past events believed to be interfering with a person's present mental and emotional wellness.
† Tony's garage was underneath his apartment with Leela. To start his not-quiet Dodge Challenger there was to insure that Leela would hear it and come to his aid.

Jerry's First Time Ever

Do you remember the first time you played with Tony, how it sounded, and how that affected your playing?

Yes! And it was like being surrounded by guitars, only it's one guy. I was listening to him more than I was to me.

But he …

He was …

He was like …

I'll just say, when Sam Bush was playing rhythm, and Crowe was playing banjo, Tony was like a tornado. And you're in the eye of the tornado but there's this guitar, it's surrounding you and it's everywhere, but it's not playing what you're playing. It's supporting you in every possible way.

His guitar wasn't just an up-and-down, fill-in-the-holes kind of rhythm. He was playing all around you. He heard every note you played and would play something to complement you: he never destroyed your solo. He didn't or overdrive his influence in your solo.

I've never played with another guitar player who did that to me, who could be so many things at once, could lead me into something that I wanted to play, or influence me to play something that I hadn't thought of playing.

Tony, at 48, styling Rush Limbaugh tie, tie bar, tie tack and Accutron watch
Backstage at the Mystic Theater, Petaluma California
February 21, 1999

Leela – Breaking up was hard to do

Leela's name has been mentioned a few times, so let's take a moment to look at her. On September 28, 1980, as an ordained minister in the Universal Life Church, I officiated Tony's marriage to his second wife, Leela Suh Satyendra, a talented, sharp, petite and beautiful lady with dark eyes and hair. He was 29; she, 28. The wedding party that followed, at a restaurant in Tiburon, included Leela's sister Gita and mother Hija, as well as Tony's mother Dorothy, as I recall.

Cupid's fletcher had crafted carefully; his arrow of true love had found Tony's heart. Tee told Peter Rowan that Leela was "the great love of his life." But the union was short-lived. Leela left their Corte Madera Avenue bungalow in the spring of 1984 and petitioned for divorce on December 19, 1985. (The dissolution document shows that Tony completed 11th grade, which coincides with Steve Swan saying that Tony quit school at 16 and left home.) When the couple's dissolution was finalized on May 1, 1986, it brought Tee low.

Steve said, "When I lived in Corte Madera with Tony [August 8, 1984 to August 8, 1985], the pain over Leela leaving him was such that he drank coffee, smoked cigarettes, drank beer [every day], and ate a single hamburger every other day. Tony drank all day and evening. He was sometimes just keeping a buzz going and other times getting obliterated to make the psychological pain go away for a little bit."

Ron Rice said Tee's breakup with Kate Freeman in 1979 might have started Tony's drinking, although it was light at first. John Reischman said Tee drank occasionally during his era with the Tony Rice Unit, 1980 to 1983. So Steve's is the first report I uncovered of Tony's drinking steadily.

Mark Johnson said Tony called him a number of times to come pick him up – this was December 1985 to Spring of '86. The two would drive north on US 19 from Crystal River, Florida, and Tony would cry his eyes out about the loss of his wife whom he loved so much. "He was devastated over losing her," Mark said.

In 1985, Tony wrote and recorded a song of lost love, "Never Meant to Be." He penned a number of instrumentals in his life, but this was the only song – music and lyrics – as far as I know, that he created.[19] When I asked Ron Rice if it was about Leela, he said, "Yeah, pretty much."

One evening during this torturous time, Tee came over to my Mill Valley digs for dinner, a blues cloud over his head. After a dreary meal, we watched the tube, appropriately, a film noir, until midnight. Then he took off his Beatle boots, lay down on the couch and dozed off. I put a blanket over him. He had a cup of joe before he left next morning.

Tony had hung out till he fell out. He didn't want to return to his lonely digs, and maybe he didn't want to be around the house when Leela called, or when she didn't call. Steve Swan said, "He never really got over Leela. He was in deep mourning for several years."

Dawg saw Big Mon[*] around this time and related Tee's funk over his ended marriage. Monroe reflected on this for the length of a chop[†] and, with the poetic brevity for which he is famous, said, "The little lady brought the big man down."

Which she had.

---

[*] Bill Monroe's nickname
[†] In bluegrass, a chop is a short, clipped after-beat often played on the mandolin.

Kate Freeman, Tony's first wife
At their Kentfield home
– by Ron Rice

Leela Satyendra, Tony's second wife
At Disney World, Orlando, early 1980s
– by Vicki Pritchard

The Gasoline Brothers

Tee and Dawg comprised a duo called the Gasoline Brothers, or the Diesel Brothers, or maybe the Gazoil Brothers (*Gazoil* is French for diesel fuel). Whatever the name, the two burned some hot bluegrass together, and issued one album I'm aware of.

Mark Schatz, Tony's bassist in the Tony Rice Unit from 1985 to 1990, told me of a dream Tony had about David.

"Now this is wild. It speaks to the kind of ego Tony had, that helped with the discipline he had to get as good as he did. He told this story on stage at the Station Inn [in Nashville] one night.

"Tony said, 'I had a dream last night. I was playing with Grisman, and I made a mistake, and Grisman turned around and shot me.'"

Mark continued, "And I thought, *Wow, there's a window into Tony.*"

I said, "Mark, one theory of dreams is that the dreamer is the writer, the director and all the actors in the dream. In that case, who was really shooting him? Was he shooting himself?"

"Yeah, I believe what you're saying. Grisman was an authority figure, so in a way it was Tony's own authority that was saying, 'I've gotta play this right. There are consequences for not getting it right. There are no allowances for not playing it right.'

"Tony Rice was immaculate."

This is a photo essay of the Diesel Brothers I'm calling "Smoke Gets in your Eyes," shot backstage in 1978 at a Northern California venue. Tony, playing his Ovation Legend, was 27, and David, holding a Lloyd Loar signed Gibson F-5 mandolin, was 33.

I notice this about these pix:
  The guitar is *always* in Tony's hands.
    He's *always* holding the flatpick.
      He doesn't puff.
        He mugs.
          He laughs.
            He smiles for the camera.

              Smiling … the Tony Rice I remember.

Jay hands something to Dawg.

David appears to puff on – I'm not sure what – maybe a cigarette.

Mary laughs long and loud.

The cameraman is offered a puff.

"No thanks!" Whadaya mean "No thanks"?

Smoke gets in you eyes.

Would ya believe this guy!

Portrait: Diesel Brothers with Nine-Finger Chord

Outtake from the original DGQ album photo shoot
Todd Phillips, the author, David Grisman, Darol Anger, Tony
– photo by Robert Schleifer

The DGQ

The DGQ usually dressed for the gig in creased cotton slacks and button-up, collared stage shirts of our own choosing. Tee was usually more dressed up than the rest of us, often styling a sport coat. It's possible Tony picked up his dress code from trumpeter Miles Davis, a sharp dresser, who learned it from cornetist Buddy Bolden,* the "first man of jazz" and first jazz man of sartorial splendor. Ron Rice suggested, "Tony's dress code, stage stance, bent knee, approach to the stage mic, and even the way he held his guitar, points to Gordon Lightfoot."

That seems right, but clips of Gordon in concert usually see him in a white stage shirt or, less frequently, a sport coat. I haven't seen concert video of him in coat and tie, which was commonly Tony's "showtime" dress, and Miles Davis'. Maybe Tony took cues from both Gordon and Miles.

I played bass behind Tony and Peter Rowan when they duo-ed at the second Freight & Salvage, at 1111 Addison Street in Berkeley. Peter wore a three-piece, bespoke suit – well, it looked made-to-order – and offhand I'd never seen Peter suited up before or since.

Tee's presence in a band was capable of boosting the group's stage dress. But a group could also ignore Tony's dress code, and take the stage sporting whatever they'd put on that morning.

---

* I write about attending Buddy's belated funeral in my book *Acoustic Stories: Pickin' for the Prez and Other Unamplified Tales*

Backstage

When he arrived in the dressing room, Tony put his Mark Leaf guitar case down on a table, and leave it there, unopened, for a few minutes. Then, with his back to the room and the goings-on it tempted, he'd slide his hands to the outer latches and open them simultaneously. He'd crack the case, let it stand for a few minutes before opening it fully for a few more, and finally take the instrument out to change strings.

He once said, "I can tell how well a man plays by how he opens his case."

With that remarkable statement, I started watching how folks *did* open their cases.

Backstage, before each gig, Tee installed a new set of strings. He'd play them for a while, re-tune, stretch them out, and repeat until show time. Every gig saw new strings … well, every one I witnessed.

On Stage

We'd take the stage for the first set and play two or three tunes before David introduced the band to the audience. Knowing my taste for the bubbly, he'd announce me as "Champagne Bill Amatneek," and I'd introduce him as "David Grass Grisman."

When he came to Tee, he usually said something about "the young master of the guitar." Tony was certainly both masterful and young. It was difficult to watch him age during the last decades of his life. The young became the old in front of our eyes. His cover pic on the March, 2021, *Bluegrass Unlimited,* by Scott Simontacchi,[20] is a sadly revealing close-up. His IBMA Hall of Fame Acceptance Speech[21] in September of 2013 was tough to watch because of how he looked, emaciated, and sounded, raspy. I'm fortunate to have played with him when he was brimming with mid-twenties energy.

As I spoke with various folks who worked with him, it was interesting to hear what each thought Tony's "Golden Age" was. Some said the DGQ years, some said it was before that, the J.D. Crowe years. Many folks were partial to The Bluegrass Band era, others to his time with Rowan & Rice, still others to the Tony Rice Unit. Each seemed to think that his or her time working with Tony was hiss golden age. So I'm not going to say it was the original DGQ years that heard the apex of Tony's playing, but he was young, bursting with ideas, and CrossFit muscular in his picking.

On stage, every tune heard a re-tuning. I'm not suggesting this is a revolutionary act. But it was the first thing Tony did when a number ended: turn away from the mic and tune up. He tuned by ear, and when finished he'd play all the first-position guitar chords, E, A, D, G and C major. They were equally in tune, a neat feat he pulled off in record time.

He used his capo – a one-off made for him by Tom McKinney – not only as a transposing tool, as all guitarists do, but also as a tuning device. He'd slap on the McKinney, and latch it just south of, say, the second fret. He'd tighten it a tad, jog it, repeat, and finally tighten it to *just* stop all the strings from buzzing, but not so much as to go sharp. Then he'd fine-tune the individual string or two that needed help, again, in record time.

Tony had beautiful ears.

When I played in the DGQ, Tony flat-picked very hard, surely causing the lateral epicondylitis (tennis elbow) he suffered, plus tendinitis and osteoarthritis in his right hand. He was a burning player, complexly urging the beat along relentlessly, the engine in any rhythm section he played in, I'm sure. It's easy to focus on Tony's left hand, and I will, but his right hand was the power behind his compelling comping, and the genesis of his tone.[*]

With this hand, Tony executed what guitarist Howard Roberts called the "spin-drive" method. Tee held the pick between

---

[*] You could argue that his tone also derived from his left hand strongly pinning down the strings to the fingerboard, and I'd agree. But this ability is shared by many guitarists. Tee's right-hand technique, on the other hand, was unique.

his thumb and the upper side of his curled-in index finger, like most folks. But most guitar pickers flat-pick from the wrist and/or forearm. Tony moved his thumb, flat-pick and index finger as an independent unit. Squiggling this unit around furiously, like writing with pen on paper, Tee got all over the strings, popping them with his tortoiseshell pick.

Most flatpickers alternate up- and down-strokes of the pick: down on the beat, up on the after-beat. It's a pattern they reliably repeat. But there is a difference between the two strokes in the angle of attack and the volume and tone they produce. Tony didn't adhere to a strictly up-down pattern; he could choose the direction of any stroke at will, pulling the tone he wanted out of any individual stroke I don't believe he was consistent with this. His choice of up- and down-strokes for a given passage of a tune could change from one execution to the next, according to how he wanted the notes to sound.

Tony didn't anchor his wrist to the guitar like some pickers; it was arched out a tad. His hand being away from the instrument, untethered to the guitar's top, allowed him to put the full weight of his forearm behind an attack.

J.D. Crowe said, "The thing I loved most about his playing was his rhythm. He's the best rhythm guitarist I've ever played with, and I've played with some good ones."[22] Tony's rhythm *was* his right hand.

Tee's first guitar lesson was "Attack the note." Tony attacked the note harder than anyone in the known universe, a large part of what made his tone unique. He jumped on it, ripped it, whipped it. No one attacked the note like Tee, not that I've heard. He throttled the notes with his tortoiseshell pick, flogging the instrument to its limits.

Bassist Charles Mingus titled one of his compositions, "Gunslinger Bird." "Bird" was the nickname of altoist Charlie Parker, an influential bebop player. Mingus gave this tune a long subtitle: "If Charlie Parker was a Gunslinger, There'd be a Whole Lot of Dead Copycats." There are Tony Rice guitar copycats around who've learned some, maybe many of his licks. What separates most of them from Tee is that they do not play with the attack that Tony had in the original DGQ era ... again, not that I've heard.

In the late '60s, I asked guitarist Gabor Szabo why he played a Martin D-45 acoustic, in an era when all jazz guitarists played electrics (and still do). He said, "Because it sounds like a guitar!"

Yes, a Martin Dreadnought sounds like a guitar in full. But such an instrument must be worked; the player must craft a fine-tuned meeting of hands and guitar to elicit tone. An acoustic, steelstrung Dreadnought is a test of the guitarist. It's an instrument that holds volumes of sounds inside it, waiting to be brought out.

With an acoustic guitar, unlike an electric, sustained notes, volume, and tone don't come easily; they're earned via long hours in the woodshed, where Tee lived back in the DGQ days.

Tony's attack made the guitar sing out, and pushed the instrument to its vibrational limits. In this, he brought sounds out of the Martin Dreadnought that hadn't been heard before. He flailed on chorded tone clusters of open and fretted strings, their tonal dissonances ringing against each other, the instrument reverberating with a roar of tones and overtones, the clicking of the pick on the strings, and the slapping of the strings on the frets and the fingerboard.

His guitar mastery rested on his precision in playing. Composer and band leader Sun Ra said, "Art does not begin with imitation, but with discipline." Tony was disciplined, He stood stock still – even when the music rocked – to create precision, but his playing had undeniable emotional content. It's this emotive force I remember. His monstrous chops let him deliver what his imagination heard.

Most folks I asked said they did not know Tony well. Knowing someone means they've shared their intimate, inner, private selves with you. Tony mostly kept his feelings to himself, it's fair to say. But he shared intimate stories with me on two occasions. It was memorable that he shared them, and memorable for what he chose to share.

As we know, some guys yarn about their sexual encounters, their "conquests." It puts us on guard, doesn't it? We may suspect the story is an empty boast. Tee confided in me on this subject, not to boast but to release the emotional intensity of the encounters, get them off his chest. One liaison was with a woman, apparently a great beauty, he met on a tour of Japan, and the other was with the girlfriend of one of the boys in the band. (For better or worse, infidelities happen in the band business, especially when the players are young.)

With both stories, related years apart, his telling of the liaison's intensity was expressed with intensity in his voice and gestures. I heard that Tony burned for these two women, as they did for him, something he also expressed.

Federico García Lorca said, "To burn with desire and keep quiet about it is the greatest punishment we can bring on ourselves." Tee could not keep quiet about it. I sensed both times that when the telling was over, he felt relief at having unburdened himself of the story. Tony was attractive to women; they desired him as only a Guitar God can be desired. Kari Estrin arranged Tony's 1985 tour of Japan, was his manager, and accompanied him on the tour. She told me this story.

"Tony was like a god in Japan – it was like he strode in right out of a Western – tall, towering over almost anyone else (Tony was 6′ 2″), blondish hair, all unique over there. The translators were very professional, but in hearing about a day when no one was working, they couldn't wait to try their chances … first making sure with me I wasn't Tony's girlfriend. … But believe it or not, Tony wasn't as interested as one might think. [He gave] them my U.S. business phone number in the states as his own, which confused several Japanese women calling to speak to Tony, with no Tony in sight. Women in the U.S. did buzz around Tony like bees to honey. We all had to get used to it on the road."

"He had an eye for the ladies," Mark Schatz said. Yes, Tony could be a skirt-chaser, one who did not get turned down a lot, I sense. Pierre Bensusan, the extraordinary finger-picking, DADGAD* guitarist, told me this story.

"I was opening for the David Grisman Quintet at the Bottom Line in New York, on my first U.S. tour back in 1979. Tony Rice was of course a member of the Quintet, and after my sound check, I attempted to go into my dressing room. When I turned the light on, there was Tony having sex with a woman. … This is the first time I've shared this anecdote with anyone."

Like Bensusan, most everyone I interviewed told a story Tony had related to them privately, or they alone had witnessed, one they were relating for the first time. It made writing this book tricky. Without Tony around to corroborate unique stories told about him, I've had to reject some as too personal or marginally credible, while assuming others were true, even though they were often "single-source" stories, the scourge of good journalism.

We all compartmentalize things we say and to whom we say them, only with Tony, like many other things he did, it feels like it was more so. Here's a story Peter Rowan told me about something personal Tony shared, likely with him alone.

* DADGAD refers to an alternative tuning of the guitar's strings. See https://en.wikipedia.org/wiki/DADGAD

"Tony wouldn't fly, so he would often drive with somebody he was sponsoring in the AA [Alcoholics Anonymous] 12-step program. He wanted to bring that person with him and they would come down to Texas. But in one of those drives across the country he was alone.

"There is this 'brotherhood of the road' kind of thing. You might hear from a musician friend who was in some other part of the world and was just touching base. I remember I was out in my cabin, living in Inverness on the coast at the time, and the phone rang at two or three in the morning and it was Tony calling from somewhere in Arizona.

"And he said 'Pete, I gotta tell you, I'm standing on the land my father bought in 1948.'

"His father had bought a little lot in the Arizona desert from the back of *Field & Stream* or some other magazine. Tony had never seen it. He was calling based purely on his emotions and intuitions. He wanted to tell me where he was. He said, 'I'm standing right on the land my dad bought.'

"And that really hit me because it was an unusual communication. He had a tough relationship with his father. In fact, he had reconnected with his father from this little piece of land Herb had bought from the back of a magazine way long ago, maybe when Tony was born. It was like all the years slipped away and emotionally he was connecting things up. And that he called to tell me that was very moving to me."

The intimacies Tony shared during these moments seemed needful. Like the 3 AM phone call to Peter, the phone call to Jerry Douglas, and the liaisons he related to me, Tee had to get them off his chest … *now.* I sensed that in many of the stories folks told me.

Back to Precision

During the sound check for a gig at U.C. Berkeley's venue, the Bear's Lair, on May 3, 1977, Tony was standing to the side of the stage, guitar strapped on, about to light a cigarette. He held it to his mouth with his left hand. In his right hand, he somehow held both the lighter and his flat-pick.

At this moment, as he was about to light up, I said, "Tee, hit me a *G*, will ya?"

There was a quarter-note rest as Tony visualized it. Then, without looking, he flicked his right hand down at the guitar and popped the open *G*-string as clean and clear as he'd ever played. The note filled the room. Then he raised his right hand to his face, flicked the Bic and lit the stick.

What struck me was that he was in cigarette-lighting mode – not playing mode – but without looking down he knew exactly where the *G*-string was, and exactly how to move his arm to hit that note hard and clean.

When it was strapped on, Tee was in a constant, fixed relationship with the guitar, which put the strings in the same place relative to his body, all the time. And in those rare, waking moments when the instrument was not strapped on, I imagine Tony was still in a relationship with it: turning it over in his mind.

One afternoon while we were recording the original DGQ album at Arch Street Studios, David played back at half-speed a few seconds of a tune we'd just just laid down. Some parts were dribbling in a tad unevenly, more to the beat than on it, but not Tony's. His notes marched in lockstep, right on the beat, defining the beat. Every stroke of his pick was even.

If Tony was unhappy with his playing during a recording, if he'd made what he considered a clam, he'd stop picking and Bronx cheer into the mic, bringing the take to an end. The rest of us were more likely to overdub a clam. But Tee had the huevos, and the clout, to unilaterally abort a take if he wished.

I sensed that in his head he counted in double time, just like music teachers say you should. If the tune was counted off as "1 2 3 4," Tony was possibly thinking, "1 *an* 2 *an* 3 *an* 4 *an*." When he kicked off one of his own tunes – "Swing 51" for instance – he'd tap the tortoise on the pick guard, tight, metronomic.

We all clean our instruments after the gig, right? Tee was reverential about it. Backstage, with his back turned to the room, he'd stand his Martin on the floor of the open Leaf case and wipe down the fingerboard and strings with a clean cloth. Then the neck, top, sides, headstock, and the rest. Tony generally wasn't

Tony's apartment in Kentfield, lower right, garage directly underneath
– phographer unknown

talking with anyone else during this interlude, though talk flowed backstage after a gig.

A Gun in the Night

At 2 AM one morning we were in Tee's Dodge Challenger, cruising back to Marin from a gig. Tony was driving to his home in Kentfield; I was riding shotgun.

Suddenly Tony floored it, saying, "Get down!"

I got down, not knowing what was up.

He swerved into his driveway and killed the headlights. "Get down! Some guy hassled me at the last light and he's after me."

I know that while driving around, things happen that only the driver sees. Guys can be competitive in their cars, and conflicts flare up suddenly, often to the ignorance of passengers. So I took Tony's word for it and slouched down, the back of my head against the door's armrest. I looked over and saw his hand holding a revolver, backlit by the moonlight against a cobalt sky.

I was hoping the bad boy would cruise by; a 2 AM shootout in this tony Marin County neighborhood would have been tacky. Fortunately, he did. Tony cooled the heat, we exited his car, and trooped inside.

The original SCGC Tony Rice Model guitar
Photo courtesy of Gryphon Stringed Instruments

The SCGC Tony Rice Model Guitar

On June 13, 1978, Tony and I drove down to Santa Cruz to pick up the first Tony Rice Model guitar from the Santa Cruz Guitar Company (SCGC), founded in 1976 by Richard Hoover, Will Davis, and Bruce Ross. This Dreadnought-sized instrument picked up one distinguishing feature of the 1935 Clarence White Martin, its oversized sound hole — the circular cutout in the guitar's top. But otherwise, SCGC's Tony Rice Model guitar is *not* a Clarence White Martin copy.[23] It is its own dreadnought.

There are multiple stories about this enlarged O-hole, but Harry Sparks' explanation, sent to me in an email, seems the most credible. "Either Tony or Clarence White said that there had been pick wear just above the pickguard that had chewed out the wood to the first line of purfling. To make the hole round again, someone carved or filed out the rest of the wood all the way around. I'm not sure who did it."

But another thing: there's a pellet gunshot hole in the Clarence White Martin on the upper bout, below the nineteenth fret. Roland said that Clarence and LeRoy McNees (a.k.a. "Mack"), the Kentucky Colonels' dobroist, were in a cabin at Big Bear Lake, California, one night, hanging out, drinking beer.

The guitar was standing up against a wall. A pellet gun was in Clarence's hand. He said, "I hate that guitar," took aim, and shot it.

Roland White gave me Mack's phone number. I called him and

asked, "Why did Clarence say he hated the guitar?"

He laughed and said, "I know it was hard to play. That's probably why."

This is another example of the instrument's high action, first noted by Kenney Music Company, following it around. In any case, the gunshot hole in the Clarence White Martin was not replicated in the SCGC Tony Rice Model guitar.

When we got back to Tee's home in Kentfield, Tony started playing the new instrument, and right away he heard something wrong. "It don't sound right. It don't feel right," he said. "Something's off."

It sounded fine to me, although like Sam Bush, I believe Tony could make any Dreadnought sing.

He reached to fret some first position notes with his left hand, and said, "Something's the matter; the notes ain't there."

Tony made them sound "there" to me.

He measured the string length from nut to bridge on the Clarence White Martin, and then he measured it on the SCGC Tony Rice model.

The string length was 1/8th inch longer on the Santa Cruz than on the Martin. Tony could feel the 1/8th inch and the string tension it added; he could hear the tonal difference.

The folks at the Santa Cruz Guitar Company made the changes Tee wanted, and continued to evolve the instrument to his tone specifications and changing physical needs over the years, creating a dozen personal custom guitars for him between 1978 and 2015. The midrange and treble in particular were fine-tuned to Tee's liking. The Tony Rice Model is SCGC's bestselling Signature Model guitar, I believe.

Every year SCGC's Richard Hoover generously donates one of their guitars to the California Bluegrass Association (CBA), which in turn raffles it off to its members, providing funds for this much-deserving group. *Thank you, Richard.*

Interior label for the first SCGC Tony Rice Model guitar
Photo courtesy of Gryphon Stringed Instruments

Pickin', Singing, Teaching & Leading

How Tony got around a steel-strung Dreadnought was unique. His technique on the guitar exploded what was being done on the Dreadnought.

Tony's Ears

Meticulous playing begins with intense listening, and Tony had big ears, "golden ears." I think his high-end was particularly acute. When we rehearsed, he listened intently, often with eyes closed.

To feed his listening habit, Tony owned three Grado cartridges for his Sony turntable, in an era when they cost $300 each (about $1,625 in 2024 dollars). He placed a turntable weight over the LP he was spinning to improve bass response, tighten the mids and highs. He was no fan of CDs when they came along, feeling the sampled sound was treble rich and chopped up.

He turned on his amplifier and demonstrated with an A/B test of the original DGQ LP versus CD. On his high-end, sound-spectrum-filling system – as high-end as home systems got – you could hear the diff. The CD's sonorities were choppy … digitized.

Playing Changes

He was innovative in how he approached playing changes. He anticipated the arrival of a new chord by a measure, creating a tension that was relaxed only when the rest of the band caught up.

He could work the climb from I to IV chord, anticipate or drag its arrival to cliff-edge effect.

Tony's Soloing

His solo work, in particular his playing fretted notes up the neck against open strings below, was innovative. He would interweave picking single strings, cross-picking, sweeping the strings, hammering-on, pulling-off, unchoking choked notes, playing barred and 4-finger chords and clusters, while occasionally using the bare middle and ring fingers of his right hand along with the flatpick,[24] all while gracefully skating the length of the fretboard. Tony knew, really knew, the guitar fretboard.

His solos were exuberant, exhilarating. We applaud a Tony solo for how deftly he renders his choice of notes. But we also feel the emotional ride he's taken us on, sometimes a roller coaster of bodily reactions: accelerated breathing, racing heart, held breath, and stunned, slack-jawed gasping.

The effect of Tony's soloing, of all his playing, was extra-musical. Mark Schatz called it "magic … high art." Béla called it being taken on the "magic carpet ride."

Play every solo "like it's the last solo you're ever going to play," Tony told Jerry Douglas.[25] And he did. Tee put everything he owned into his breaks. His choruses built to climaxes that whooshed through the last 16th note with a ridiculously forceful G-run, leaving the next soloist with a hypersonic rocket to captain.

Peter Rowan said, "It's funny. He'd blister a solo and then look over at me and say, 'Go wild, man!' and he meant it!"

A Tony Rice chorus was a hard act to follow. Peter continued, "At the first MerleFest, I noticed all of those people sitting out there on hay bales, and when Tony took a solo there was this collective intake of breath that was audible.

"Wherever he showed up where people really weren't used to

his delivery, like in Texas, it would be the same thing. The people around Austin when we played the Old Settlers Festival, there would be this collective gasp when Tony finished his solo.

"He pushed his mortal boundaries as far as he could. He had a complicated karma with his extended family. He had dreams of soaring … My own fear of flying was challenged," Peter said.

Tony's Singing

Tee was easily one of the top three bluegrass singers of his era. His voice, when it deserted him, when it turned to gravel – likely accelerated by singing higher than his natural baritone – was sorely missed by his adoring public, but mostly by him, of course.

He lost more than his singing. Steve Swan said, "The loss of the wide array of funny voices and characters was an even greater loss to him, socially, than the loss of his gorgeous singing voice." The characters included cabdriver Bill Snowden, whom we'll meet shortly.

One theory is that Tee did this to himself, that he self-abused his voice until it deserted him. Here's my take on it, and I don't believe I'm alone. After my time with the group, the DGQ acquired a band saying, "Hey Mang." (We'll hear more about this soon.) He started producing this phrase from the back of his throat, growling it. The growl slowly spread to everything he spoke.

In his 2013 IBMA acceptance speech – the event also saw his last public performance on guitar – he spoke in his graveled voice about recently trying a few things to see if anything could happen towards its restoration.

"If my Heavenly Father is willing … I might be able to show you a little bit of what I've been working on. This is not easy."

He Clinch Mountain back-steps* from the mic, hums a low note,

---

* "Clinch Mountain Backstep," a banjo instrumental by Ralph Stanley, adds an odd beat to the B-section of the tune, a "backstep."

steps back up, and resumes talking normally, though very softly. "Now I am speaking in my real voice," he whispers.

The audience breaks into applause with some in the room rising to their feet, a moment that Jerry Douglas commented on.

Ron Rice told me that in the years following the IBMA speech, Tee's voice went through good periods and bad.

Tony as Teacher

Ron Rice put Tony's friend, Mark Johnson, in touch with me. Mark lived in Dunnellon Florida, as did the Rice family from 1966-67. In the '80s and '90s, Tony worked with Mark on his music, taught him how to listen intently, how to accompany. I asked Mark to write his remembrances of Tony's teaching, and feel very fortunate he did. *Thank you, Mark.*

"On the many weekend evenings when we were not driving through the night, we would sit in his home on the water behind Charlie's Fish House Restaurant in Crystal River, Florida.

"He was a nocturnal guy and would be waking up around seven or eight PM in the evenings, and give me a call to come on over. He had the most amazing collection of LPs along with a fantastic stereo system. The shelving unit was horizontal and measured about six to eight feet long with two rows of LPs. The top shelf was all acoustic/New Grass/bluegrass/folk records, and the bottom shelf was all jazz LPs.

"Tony and I would spend many evenings together just listening to specific LPs that he liked and wanted me to hear. He would direct me to pick out specific instruments on a recording and listen for things he would question me on to see if I picked up on it.

"He would get up off the couch and place an LP on a turntable and say, "Let's listen to this piece of music." It was a jazz album, and I was nervous because he would just kick back on the couch and close his eyes and listen.

"When I first tried doing this, I couldn't keep quiet more than a minute or two. And he would open his eyes and look at me and shush me to be quiet, which made more nervous. But I was able to settle down and focus on what we were listening to.

"After a while he would change out the LPs to listen to other jazz musicians. I recall listening to a cut of his hand-signed Miles Davis LP when he stopped it and said, "I want you to listen to just the bass player in this piece and then tell me what you hear."

"The more I listened specifically to the bass player, the more I became aware of how that musician was feeling his way through a piece. I could hear his fingers quietly working the fingerboard and sometimes hear him breathing, but more importantly, I heard how the bass player was pulling tone out of his instrument, how he was emoting.

"I remember him pulling out a two-track reel-to-reel tape recording of J.D. Crowe sitting in a wooden chair, playing a solo version of "Colored Aristocracy" and when the recording was over, he asked me what I had heard.

"I told him I heard everything from J.D.'s fingers moving across the strings, a thumb pick hitting the banjo head and the amazing tone that he was pulling on his banjo. But when I said to Tony that I had heard the wooden chair creak, that was when he took out his guitar and said, "Get your banjo out."

"From then on, we would play old fiddle tunes and swap playing the lead and backup melodies back and forth, often playing off each other's take on the melody. I found out that the more I listened to him play his take, the more I would take his cue and start playing the melody more instinctively.

"I learned that backup playing is in fact another form of playing lead using countermelodies and harmonies. It was amazing how far we took this music.

"Tony taught me how to not only understand working with other musicians, but to also create my own music. It was in late 1992 that we all got together to record my *Clawgrass* album with my own original music."

Tony's photo from the 1966 Dunnellon High School class year book
– photographer unknown

Tony as Band Leader

Tony commanded acute stage skills as front man: band leading, tempo setting, musical directing, lead singing, minimal emceeing – he didn't like to talk on stage; thanks for that lesson, Tee – and maximum music.

He pulled off the band leader gig like no one else, and was a lesson in how to lead a bluegrass band on stage. Watching the 1988 MerleFest videos,[26] we see Tony as Band-Wrangler-in-Chief, masterfully – with a flick of his eyes – herding into the Tony Rice stampede a group of strong and headstrong musicians, Sam Bush, Béla Fleck, Mark O'Connor, Jerry Douglas, all leaders in their own right, all under Tony's leadership, and all anchored by string bassist Mark Schatz.

Tony Rice Unit: Jimmy Gaudreau, Tony, Mark Schatz, Wyatt Rice circa 1987
photo courtesy of Mark Schatz
– photographer unknown

Mark Schatz Speaks

Mark Schatz played in the Tony Rice Unit from 1985 to 1990. We talked at my home on March 10, 2022.

Mark, how do you remember Tony?

M ark, how do you remember Tony?
He was a unique, charismatic dude. His take on things, his perception of things, his world view, were all unusual. He would always tell you how he felt about things, and it was always a little bit different; the take he had on something was often a little weird.

He liked to do things well and right. He dressed well, whether he was informal or formal. The time I was with him he generally had a coat and tie. He liked his nice clothes. He was fastidious: hair done right, and always clean and squared away.

He liked good quality stuff. He was one of the first ones to have a DAT Walkman cassette player. He was also into photography and had some really nice cameras. Kind of obsessive. Part of that formal thing: he had a beautiful Lincoln town car he drove when I knew him. He liked his creature comforts.

He had this kind of posture, a little bit stiff, a little formal. When he came into a room he had natural presence, but formal in a way. His regular demeanor wasn't exactly relaxed and "Hey let's hang out." There was always a kind of a formality to the exchanges. When he got to drinking, smoking, he loosened up.

Talking to him was not like you and me talking to each other.

It was this kind of oblique thing with Tony. I never felt really at ease with him … and I played music with him.

It's not to say he didn't have warmth. There was some real personal warmth and generosity of spirit as well. When my late wife, Eileen, got sick, I got him on the phone. And he spent a long time with me just really talking about that, and extending. And he said, "I got this feeling that she's going to be all right." I mean really warm and optimistic and loving. As weird as he can be and as distant as he can be, there was also that side; you could feel that.

As the years went by, I understood that when you're playing with somebody, you don't really see the forest for the trees. I wondered if he was on the Asperger's spectrum.* Not being disparaging about that in any way, but sometimes there was a little awkwardness in social interactions.

He could be obsessive with things. Everybody knew this about Tony. He got some expression he would say, and he could say it over and over and over again.

Another thing: he was not a self-promoter in any way at all, to his detriment, I think. It's almost like this old school approach – "Look, I'm just going to do the things I do and if people like 'em, that's great."

Sometimes when he would talk about CDs from the stage, he would say something like, "We have some jars of kumquat jam that Mark's grandmother made." It was just some Tony humor, and maybe a touch of disdain for having to lower himself to hawk CDs. For the record, my grandmother did not make kumquat jam.

Not long after starting to work with him, we recorded *Me and My Guitar*. Listening to the depth of emotion of his vocals, I thought, *Man, this guy has something going on, something really special happening. Let's promote this record. Let's push it. Let's get*

---

* Asperger syndrome, a.k.a Asperger's, is an autism spectrum disorder, a neurobiological syndrome affecting social and communication skills.

a manager. That's what I was about.

And Tony was, "I dunno. Maybe." We set up a meeting with a guy who was a well-known manager in Nashville. Tony showed up late, inebriated, and that was the end of that.

When I said, "Tony, let's do some record promotion, some radio stuff," Tony said, "Nah, we just put it out there. If people like it, they'll buy it." Almost like anti-business. I'm sure he liked the royalties and everything. But it was kind of an organic approach: just put it out there, let people hear it and have their own opinions about it. Why should we do any special promotion or pushing?

It's not the best when you're trying to build your career. But he didn't really have a career path that I knew of. Never talked much about it. Never happened. But maybe it did: Get out there and play the gigs and try to keep myself in the manner to which I am accustomed.

I know his father was a musician and introduced his boys to music. He was also a pretty bad alcoholic. I once saw a drunk father treating his child abusively, and wondered if Tony received any abusive treatment from his father that could have hurt him. I'm guessing there's a lot of pain in there as a result of this.

How did you know that?

Tony's drinking. He seemed like a tortured artist in a way. Sometimes anger is a great motivator for art, I've heard.

To be a great musician, you've got to have the motivation, which can come from a lot of different sources – love of the music, of course, and sometimes from pain, anger, needing to prove something to someone. Tony likely had a combo of these which compelled him to practice the way he did. He was passionate about music. He loved it. When he was practicing that guitar, he was like driven to ecstasy. Anger, and a somewhat obsessive personality were parts of that.

Jazz

He played bluegrass but he loved jazz. Just loved it, had a reverence for it. He took certain tonalities and harmonic stuff from jazz, and included it as part of his artistry, as part of his playing: the suspended chords, the extended chords. I think he got some schooling from John Carlini in jazz harmony and phrasing. I don't think anyone ever thought of him as a jazz guitarist. On his duo CD with John, you can hear the contrast between a legit jazz guy and Tony's unique approach to those kinds of tunes on that recording.

Any situation where you can hear everything Tony is doing laid bare, is cool. That was something nice about the duo with Peter Rowan they had for many years. You heard a lot of Tony's guitar, all that incredible, complex backup. His rhythm playing alone is masterful artwork.

He had a very strong ego. And sometimes he'd say, "That ain't shit," or disparage something. But generally not people. He had a good sense of humor. He could tell a good joke.

I loved the guy, spent a lot of time on the road with him, and had as much a relationship as you can have with somebody who was as quirky and hard to get close to as him. There was affection between us, I thought. He cared about me as much as he could, in his way. There was definitely that. But it wasn't like a good friend with whom you have a good rapport. I guess love has different forms.

Was he still despondent about Leela when you knew him?

It was my understanding that the breakup with Leela sent him into a terrible depression. And part of what helped get him out of it was Kari Estrin who went to Tony and said, "Hey, Tony, let's get you some gigs." She set things up, and once there were the gigs – Tony always lived for the gigs – I guess he got up, and it wasn't long after that I joined the Tony Rice Unit.

Then everybody wanted to hear Tony sing. I don't know how

long he was out of it with his dark depression. But when he came back from that, one of the things Kari said was, "Hey, people want to hear you sing. I can get you gigs doing that, and make some money. What do you think?"

I guess he was ready to do that again. He moved back to the east coast; a lot of the gigs were back there; he had family there, and maybe he had to put some distance between himself and his difficult breakup in California.

Mark Joins the T.R.U.

My first gig with the Tony Rice Unit was at The Birchmere in Alexandria, Virginia. Up till then, Todd Philips [on bass] had done almost everything with Tony. Jimmy Gaudreau told me Todd couldn't do it for some reason or other and asked if I wanted to do the gig. So, I said, "Yeah, I'll play with Tony Rice." I learned his stuff and played the gig.

After the gig, Tony called and said, "Hey, you want to play some more shows with me?"

I was reticent at first because I had my own career path of trying to get established in Nashville with a country singer or act.

Tony said, "Well that's all right. I'll just give you a call the next time there's a gig, and if you can do it, come do the gig with me." It was very quirky. Normally if someone of his stature calls a player and they express any hesitation, there would be no more calls. It was such a loose and kind of flexible approach. For a full-time band, it was unusual.

So I said "Fine," and he called me the next time there was a gig, and I was available for the next three or four or five he called me for.

I had this epiphany: What was I looking for in country music? I was looking for a good singer, some road gigs, and it would be great if there was some good playing going on as well in the band.

Mark Schatz, Tony, Sam Bush

– venue, date and photographer unknown

And I went, Holy shit. Here's this incredible singer, here's some incredible playing. It's not in the genre I'd been in. But … I was all in at that point. You're on your path; sometimes you know to jump ship … immediately.

Tony is tremendously loyal. When he hires someone, he keeps them. When you're playing with him, you'll most likely be recording with him. That's a really great trait.

In the end, a number of factors led to my departure from the band. Tony's drinking was becoming more of a problem. As the road manager I would be the one trying to get him out of bed in the morning from time to time. I was also the one interfacing with the agent, arranging travel, advancing gigs, etc. Tony liked staying in nicer hotels, so we all stayed where he stayed. It was kind of a socialist organization in that way. It was a pretty smooth running machine.

Then the band got a new member who became Tony's drinking buddy. He had ideas about how the band should be run which were at odds with mine, and for whatever reason Tony was open to this. I felt like it undermined the functioning of the band, and I felt kind of pushed aside as well. This all contributed to my growing inclination to make an exit from the band.

There had been offers to join other bands through the years. But when I was with Tony, I said, "No, that isn't going to get me away from Tony Rice."

Then I heard that Tim O'Brien was leaving Hot Rize and going off to do his own thing. And I'd always been a big fan. Tim was this opportunity: a beautiful singer and songwriter, a great player. This was enticing.

And I went to Tony and said, "Well, I took a gig with Tim. I'll play with you for another couple of months while you find another guy."

I think it knocked him for a loop when I quit. I did it unceremoniously and with no thought of how it might affect him. It must have been a real blow to Tony, because we were close. Though the last year or so, I wasn't as connected with him because of this new band member of his.

Mark Dreams of Tony

I had a dream at one point after I left the band. Tony was on the floor and I was over him, shaking his shoulders like this ... I was mad at him for drinking, for all of the stuff that had become difficult with him in the band.

And Tony was looking up and saying, "I know. I know."

I guess this was my hurt self, acknowledging my frustration and anger, and that things had been difficult for me.

But we did have a good talk a few years later at Telluride. He'd straightened out, wasn't drinking at all at that point, and was still playing, still singing. There was some reconciliation:

"I'm sorry I did that."

"It's all OK."

It wasn't deep or complicated. There was some understanding, some reconciliation that took place. And that felt good. It's funny. You hang on to this stuff, and it takes so little to let go of it.

Did you know Tony as a toker or a drinker?

Much more as a drinker. I guess he was smoking some, but not like [he mentions someone's name]. But no, I didn't see him smoke a lot. It didn't seem like a daily thing, to me. To his credit, Tony was rarely overly inebriated when we took the stage; it was more after the gig that the imbibing could get excessive.

What was it like playing with Tony?

When he played those first few notes of a kickoff and the band jumped in, it was entering a different world where timing, taste, and tone were in perfect synch with each other. It's called a groove, and Tony's was a mile deep – you're relaxed and excited as you get swept into his world.

Tony's rhythm playing did not contain a lot of bass runs, or lines that lead from one chord to the next, typical of many acoustic guitarists.* It was a complex mixture of strums, cross picking, syncopations, and of course, Lester Flatt G-runs, at the appropriate moments and with many variations.

This left a lot of room for me to be creative with my lines, which was gratifying and edifying. And never once did he turn around and say "Hey man, don't do that." If he felt like the band's timing was off, instead of getting pissed off at us, he'd presume that we just weren't hearing well, and he'd make a little gesture with his head to me to indicate that I should come a little closer to him.

Since I was plugged in (I run a mic/pickup combo on my bass) I wasn't constrained by a mic on a stand, so I could easily accommodate. Another fond memory I have was when I'd hit a clam (a mistake – it happens to the best of us), he'd always hear it and he'd smile or chuckle a little. He was so demanding of himself, but seemed to have room for the failings of others.

Tony carried an AKG 451 microphone with him for live shows; it's a pretty brittle sounding mic, so he wouldn't record with it, but it helped get volume, tone, and clarity in a live situation. I initiated a routine where we'd get everything set up and Wyatt would check that mic for him – he got to know the tone and monitor mix Tony would want. This saved Tony from some of the tedium of sound checks in indoor venues, and in a festival setting he could remain offstage until he was announced so he could make a big entrance, stride up to the mic, and kick off the first song.

Speaking of Wyatt, I have never been a big fan of two guitars in a

---

* It makes it difficult for bassists because it leaves less room for us to play bass. – BA

bluegrass configuration, but Tony is one of the only guys who can do that. It worked in this situation for a variety of reasons. First of all, Wyatt learned to play from Tony, so there was a pretty darned close match groove-wise. They would capo in different places on their guitars so as not to be in exactly the same frequency range which helped maintain some clarity. When Tony was playing rhythm, Wyatt would hang back some, and when Tony played a kick-off or soloed, he would have a full rhythm section behind him – Wyatt, Jimmy on mandolin, and me.

Tony would throw a solo to Wyatt from time to time, and he did a great job, but it always paled next to Tony's clarity and drive, not to mention that he didn't generally have his own AKG to help get his guitar out there. I always thought it was not an enviable spot for Wyatt, but he did the job with grace and was a warm presence, and it must have felt good to Tony to have his brother on board. When I got into occasional jams with just Wyatt on guitar, he really delivered a great groove. The way we set up on stage, I had a direct line of sight to Wyatt, and now and then we'd have knowing visual exchanges. I remember one of these moments in particular.

The Unit (Tony, Wyatt, me) with special guest, a young Alison Krauss, had played the Birchmere on a Saturday night. It was a great show. The next night we had a show at a nice club in Baltimore – I think it was Blues Alley. Apparently, Tony had gone on a bender after the Birchmere show and he was not there at showtime on Sunday.

So, we got started with Alison singing some songs and doing some instrumentals. Tony showed up about 20 minutes later, quite bleary-eyed, but of course well dressed, and got up on stage with us. He played his usual collection of songs, but tempos on everything were painfully slower than usual. Wyatt and I just looked over at each other wide-eyed. Tony got some coffee in him during the break and was back up to speed for the second set.

Playing with Tony was like nothing else, but there were some frustrations. When most artists release a new recording, they typically work up a lot of that material for their live show. This helps promote the recording, it adds new energy to the band, and gives the audience something new. Tony would add only a few songs from new albums while the rest of us were chomping at the bit to play more of the recent stuff.

Tell me about recording with Tony.

I don't remember ever rehearsing for a recording session, and there was minimal discussion about arrangement once we were all gathered in the studio. He had the song meticulously worked out and arranged on the guitar; he'd play the song and count on the artistry, sensibility, and taste of those he'd called on to add the appointments to the building he had constructed.

Strangely enough, I never saw him in the process of working out an arrangement for a new song. When he presented it to us it was a *fait accompli*. He always knew the words, and played his worked-out parts pretty much flawlessly, take after take, and I don't remember us doing a lot of takes of anything – things went down pretty quickly. He sang and played everything "live," which means he rarely overdubbed his vocals. We were cutting to 2-inch tape back then, and occasionally they'd splice a couple of different takes together, but I don't recall that there was a lot of that. It was an exciting and creative process, and he rarely had any strong opinions or judgments or direction about what we played.

Jerry Douglas was on most of those sessions; his peerless backup and accompaniment sensibilities were an important part of filling out Tony's arrangements. I think the only direction I ever got from Tony was maybe on Gordon Lightfoot's "Sixteen Miles," where he wanted to hear a high pedal tone on the bass.

Tony's Singing

You've mentioned Tony's singing a few times. Tell me more.

To me, and to many in the bluegrass world, Tony's singing was as moving, unique, and compelling as his guitar playing. There are many good singers; he was a great singer. He had a unique, unmistakable tone, his phrasing was flawless, smooth, and creative. He never over-sang, but would insert some embellishment or a variation at the right moments. There was no vibrato – just a clear, direct tone.

For someone who didn't write their own songs, which was largely the case for Tony, it was all about their choice of songs. Tony had a foot in two different worlds in this regard.

There was the world of his roots in the bluegrass that he loved – Bill Monroe, Flatt and Scruggs, Jimmy Martin, the Delmore Brothers. He sang these songs like no one else, embracing the tradition, but also making them his own. There were bluegrass numbers sprinkled throughout his recordings, but he really held forth on the *Bluegrass Album Band* series,* *Tony Rice Plays and Sings Bluegrass*, and on the beloved and understated *Skaggs and Rice*.

Then there was another world of more contemporary singer/songwriters like Ian Tyson, Bob Dylan, Randy Newman, Rodney Crowell, Bob Franke, Norman Blake, and of course, Gordon Lightfoot. I believe he was first introduced to Gordon Lightfoot by an art teacher in high school, so I believe this pull toward this kind of material went way back. It's story songs like "Home From the Forest" and "Ginseng Sullivan," songs with great emotional depth like "Hard Love" and "Song for a Winter's Night," and edgy songs like "Sweetheart Like You" and "Night Flyer."

When the *J. D. Crowe & The New South* album came out in 1975, as well as ushering in the groove and sound of the next generation of bluegrass, there was some material the character of which had

---

* Mark played on Volume 5, *Sweet Sunny South*, which also featured Vassar Clements.

rarely been heard in bluegrass before including "Rock Salt and Nails," "Ten Degrees and Getting Colder," "Summer Wages," and "Home Sweet Home Revisited."

It was Tony's delivery and tone that gave these superlative songs their emotional impact. Of course, it didn't hurt to have Ricky Skaggs adding angelic tenor, and Jerry and J.D. their impeccable and colorful backup.

Tony's Guitar Playing

Then there was Tony's guitar laying down the rhythmic and intricately crafted foundation for it all. He's a monster of a guitar player, of course, but when he sings it feels like the guitar is at the service of the song.

As you know, Tony's stint with the DGQ led to a more instrumentally focused period of time for him. But with his re-emergence as the much more vocal-oriented Tony Rice Unit, the bluegrass world was once more blessed with his singing. This was around 1985, when I started playing with him.

To be honest, his voice was already showing signs of wear and tear. It was not as clear as it was in the New South days, and he didn't have the same range or control. But it was still compelling, and what may have been lost technically was made up for with deeper emotional content, evident on songs like "Hard Love" and "Shadows."

When was the last time you played with Tony?

I guess it was the last time that several of his old, beloved friends played with him, which was at IBMA in 2013, the same year he was inducted into the Bluegrass Hall of Fame. There was a concept for a set at the Red Hat Amphitheatre, which they used for big acts on the weekend. It was supposed to be all of the first year winners of IBMA awards, which included Sam, Del McCoury, Stuart

Duncan, Alison Krauss, string bassist Roy Huskey Jr., and Tony. Roy had passed away years earlier and I was the next winner so I got the call. Alison was having trouble with her singing, so she bowed out, and Stuart was not available, so Jason Carter was on fiddle. Jerry and Béla were also in the band. We had a rehearsal the day before and of course there was conjecture about whether Tony would show up for the gig; the consensus was "Not likely," and we proceeded to make a set that would likely not include him.

The next evening, we were backstage doing some warming up before our set, and to everyone's surprise Tony showed up, looking gaunt and aged, his nice suit kinda hanging off him. Still there was the question, *Is he going to play?* He seemed pretty ambivalent, and Sam told him that he was welcome to come out for as few or as many numbers he wanted to play on. We'd optimistically had a mic set up for him. Seems like he may have waited for a couple tunes before he came out, but when he did the place went wild, and we were all a bit agog as well. To all of our surprise and amazement, he stayed out for the whole rest of the set. His playing was pretty rough, but hell if he didn't hang in there, playing rhythm and taking solos.

It was sad, amazing, and surreal.

And the last time you spoke with him?

My wife of 15 years, whom I'd been with for 30, passed away in July of 2019. There had always been a good connection between them – Eileen had a way of seeing past a person's odd layers and finding the good parts of them. Tony called a couple of months later to offer his condolences and we chatted for a good while. As I stood out on my front walk in the afternoon sunshine, he offered me some advice.

He said something like, "You know, it's been psychologically proven that while you're listening to really good music, you can't feel pain at the same time." He was offering an antidote, though temporary, for the pain of my grief.

I didn't know if I necessarily agreed with him at the time, but it was sweet that he was trying to help, and maybe it's a window into what music was for him.

[Mark plays my 1875 Czech flat-back bass and longtime friend, seen here and on the original DGQ album cover]

God, it sounds so great. That's what a bass is supposed to sound like. It has so much tone. That's great. That's awesome. What a beautiful voice it has. A lot of resonance, warmth. This is rare. That thing just sounds great. You could pay $50 to $100 grand to get close to that sound.

Tony would say, "It sings like a bird."

Thanks again for coming and talking about Tony.

I appreciate your asking and being open to my input. Once I start talking, there's a lot to say. He was an enigma, really. He was not like anybody else, and affected many people's lives. He was weird, colorful, hard to know. Tony was an interesting, complicated dude.

He was a good band leader. I watch those videos [of Merlefest] with some regularity. I was looking at one the other day. It was the stature, the presence, and holding the whole thing together.

Nobody ever made playing bluegrass as easy as Tony. With time, I felt more and more moved and entranced by Tony – he was a true artist whose music could transform, move, heal, and inspire – he was magic!

Béla Fleck is a wizard of the 5-string banjo. Like Earl Scruggs and Bill Keith, his mastery of the instrument has lifted the banjo community's skill set. His decades of work, across many music genres, created a renaissance of the banjo, an instrument whose popularity had lurked for a time in the shadows of the mandolin renaissance.

His group, "Béla Fleck and the Flecktones," distinguishes him as a serious band leader, and new music creator and arranger. His work encompasses bluegrass, jazz, classical, and rock, electronic and pure acoustic sounds, as he allies himself with furiously talented musicians from many music genres, including jazz great, pianist Chick Corea.

His playing hears the influence of Scruggs, Keith, Don Reno, and Eddie Adcock. He sometimes grabs a chord up the neck, and with the right hand picks away furiously while making slight left-hand finger moves, in moments sounding like Philip Glass, only bluegrassy. He thumbs the fifth string more frequently than other folks. Like Tony, like all the greats, he gets maximum music out of minimum hand and finger movement.

Béla has won 15 Grammies in the categories of Best Folk Album, Best Country Performance, Best Bluegrass Album, Best Pop Instrumental Album, Best Contemporary World Music Album, and Best Jazz Album, demonstrating his wide eclecticism.

As we will read, Béla is a listener, a watcher, and in turn, a learner. He learned audio editing, for instance, watching Tony. And we learn about Tony listening to Béla.

We spoke via proprietary videotelephony cloudware on August 23, 2022.

Béla Fleck Speaks

Béla, how do you remember Tony Rice?

B I think about him a lot. You know, he was really funny, really weird and really smart in all his own ways. He had a lot of high esthetic, high ideals, and was a complicated human being. He was the missing link that connected bluegrass guitar playing to the next obvious place, obvious to him only. This whole set of fabulous characteristics is why we talk about him. Being complicated is part of it too.

He was an unusual kind of person who I think was very shy. I think he loved playing music with people, but deep in his core [he was] super shy. I think about how he didn't want to travel with anybody. He wanted to travel by himself, all the time, show up at the last minute, especially in his later years.

But I think that certain musicians just lit him up, people like Vassar Clements, Sam Bush, Bill Keith, and so forth. You would hear him talking about folks like that, how much he cared about them and what they did.

You too lit him up, Béla.

Well, that's good to hear. He lit me up. He could turn you on, he could make you play like nobody's business. Something about the way he did it made everybody play so much better around him. The "magic carpet ride," I call it.

He was funny; he was odd. He didn't like to practice when I knew him, though I know he practiced with the DGQ. Later on I think he preferred not to. I think he must have had a lot of hand pain that made him not want to have the guitar in his hands too much.

I remember the 1988 *Drive* album, which was a big deal for me. He played on it. He did all the live takes and stuff, but if you asked him to try and overdub another solo, he'd do it, but he'd play just one and then put the guitar back in the case and close the latches. And sometimes that first take would be absolutely perfect. He'd latch up the guitar, and I'd go, "Oh, that's … great."

Sometimes I would think to myself, "OK, you've played a lot of guitar solos on a lot of records, and I want what you play on my record to be something special."

I didn't want to say it out loud in those words, but when you're working with people who do a lot of recording, there's almost no point in working with them unless you can bring something a little bit different out of them. So I felt compelled to push him a little bit.

I think at the time it was a little irritating, but after the fact he seemed quite happy with the recordings and he would tell me again and again how much he liked them and how much he sat around and listened to the records, which of course meant a lot to me.

Do you remember the first time you met him or played with him?

I'm pretty sure the first time I played with him was when Sam Bush had cancer. Newgrass Revival was on hiatus, and there was going to be a benefit for Sam at the Great American Music Hall. This could have been the end of 1982.

So I thought, I'm sure not going to miss that. Because I'm in Newgrass Revival with Sam, I didn't think they could turn me away, and maybe I'd get to play with my heroes.

So I went out there and while I was there I asked them all if they'd help me make a duo record. All of them, including Tony, agreed. I came out and stayed on various people's couches for several weeks, including Tony's.

I worked up a piece with Tony, "Double Play," and then we did that benefit for Sam. The tune that I wrote that Tony played on was pretty incredible to do with him, but playing in a bluegrass context with him at the benefit was a high level experience for me. I was just so excited to play with Tony.

And the next time I believe was the first Merlefest, in 1988. It was Tony, Sam, John Cowan on electric bass, Mark O'Connor on fiddle, Jerry Douglas on dobro, and me. We threw together the first Merlefest jam – which was that band playing bluegrass standards, and it was incredible.[27] And then he invited me to play on *Cold on the Shoulder* either before or after that.* And that was the big one for me.

That was like, *Wow - I'm getting to record with the dudes!* Vassar was there, and Sam, Jerry, Tony, Todd, and me. We were all in one room and sang and played everything live, and did just a few takes of each song. It was amazing.

And I thought, *Wow, if I could ever get Sam, and Tony, and Jerry in a room together playing my music, that would be a dream come true.*

And that's what led me towards doing 1988's *Drive*. And then some years later, around 1999, we did that group again, on an album called *Bluegrass Sessions*.

The music was more complex. And his comment to me was always, "Too many brains, Béla. Too many brains. So many parts."

And I'd say, "Just try it, Tony. Just try it."

And we'd sit in a circle and work on these things, and then we'd go behind our mics, and lay this stuff down. And he was always a

---

* From Tony's introduction on the Merlefest cut, it seems *Cold on the Shoulder* preceded the first Merlefest.

great trouper, in terms of recording takes with the whole band. He never seemed to mind that. He just didn't really want to overdub.

Tony was the one who taught me about editing. You know how into editing he was back then. Tony had a cassette deck with an editing block where you could edit cassettes. The place the tape runs through was open to the air.

When he recorded his records he would work on the edits on cassettes before cutting the two inch tape. He would run off a bunch of cassettes of the material and practice his edits and make notes, and then he would go to Arch Street studios or whatever studio it was, and do the real edits on 2 inch, so he wasn't cutting, and re-cutting the actual 2 inch, which was scary to do.

He'd figure out what worked, and seeing him do that showed me, "Oh, there's a way to use all the great live playing magic that happened and instead of going in afterwards and overdubbing, you can take the very best stuff from each take and make a master take." That changed my whole viewpoint.

So by the time I got to *Bluegrass Sessions* I had Pro Tools,* and I was editing between takes a lot. On *Drive,* maybe we might do one edit per song on the 2 inch tape at the time, but now [with Pro Tools] it was so easy to edit, so I could really make the most out of what Tony and everybody played on the studio floor.

They'd all leave and I'd study the takes and put something together and he always delivered something fantastic. It might not have happened on the take, but it happened. That's the great thing about editing, you can use the best of what everybody did live. They really played it.

Tony Lets Béla Down

Did Tony tour with you behind any of your albums?

No, in fact he let me down a number of times in mammoth ways.

The first was when I was going to record my second banjo

---

* Pro Tools is digital audio software for sound recording and editing.

album *Natural Bridge,* and he had agreed to play guitar on it, and Grisman had agreed. Mark O'Connor was going to play fiddle – he was playing guitar in the DGQ then – and he was quite excited about playing fiddle again.

Literally the day before the session – at midnight as I remember – 'cause I was supposed to fly out there that next morning with Mark Schatz – Tony backed out.

It was too soon. I was making a play to have Tony and David play together. They had only stopped playing together in DGQ a few years before, so they hadn't worked out their personal issues.

It would have been cool for my project to have brought them back together, but Tony just wasn't ready to play with David again and he even said, "Hey man, can't you get another mandolin player?"

And it was like, "I don't think I can fire one guy cause another guy doesn't want to play with him. Especially one of my heroes!"

At any rate we rescheduled the session and O'Connor moved over to guitar and Darol Anger played fiddle. Mark was pretty pissed off about it at the time because he was playing so much guitar, and he really wanted to play fiddle. But you don't hold a grudge against your favorite musician in the world, so I forgave Tony.

The next time was after we made *Bluegrass Sessions.* We had agreed to a major tour, which was six weeks of shows, on a tour bus, and literally a few days before it began he canceled. He just backed out. Bryan Sutton saved the day and was quite capable, but it wasn't the same thing.

I never held it against Tony. I thought he was a force of nature and I didn't expect him to follow the rules of good conduct or humanity. I loved him.

It's cool that he recorded on those recordings, and all the different things we did, and he'd always ask me to play with him if I showed up where he was playing, and there was a warmth there.

Getting Branford's Autograph

I have this memory of him asking me, "Hey man, you are playing on the *Tonight Show*, right?"

"Yeah."

"You think you could get me Branford Marsalis's autograph?"

So I got him Branford's autograph, a signed photo of Branford from *The Tonight Show* when we played it with the Flecktones. When I visited Tony he had it on his mantel, next to his turntable, along with a note from me that said, "Tony, thank you for playing on my record. You played your ass off. What is it like to not have an ass anymore?"

And he had those two things on his mantel. That made me know that even though he became virtually unreachable at a certain point, that there was a warmth there; I didn't imagine it.

Do you feel you were close friends with him?

Well, it's weird. I always felt that the music was so heavy we were playing together, these experiences we would have, that there was an implied closeness. But he was a hard guy to feel close to in other ways.

He was very honest, he was very sweet, but he could be weird. The years when he was drinking were complicated. But I always felt privileged to be in his presence.

So I don't know if you could call us "friends," in the typical sense. As I talked to other people whom I assumed were close with him, I found a very similar story.

There was a distance, a disappointing distance, even though there's this incredible love at the same time. He would show it in different ways, but … it didn't mean he'd pick up the phone when you'd call him, or respond. He was very comfortable with not being responsive to people, even very close people.

But then again, Sam had his issues with Tony, but the phone

would ring on Sam's birthday, and it would be Tony calling. He would do things to let you know. Or he'd talk to you about somebody else, knowing that you might tell them. That sort of thing.

We had a yearly thing at Merlefest where we would play, and we had various all-star get-togethers, particular shows where we would put that band together. I remember gigs in Knoxville with Sam and Jerry and him. I remember playing Martinsville, Virginia, the Birchmere, etc. There were probably dozens of them.

I remember going to see him play and him dragging me on stage at little places like the Towne Crier Café in Pawling, New York. If I was there he would often ask me to come out and play.

And then in terms of recording, he played on *Double Time,* he played on *Bluegrass Sessions,* he played on *Drive.* He also played on an album called *Tales from the Acoustic Planet,* which was kind of a mixture of my bluegrass friends and my jazz friends. People like Branford and Chick Corea were on there, and the Flecktones guys were on there, but so were Sam, Jerry, and Stuart Duncan.

He played rhythm on some pretty involved stuff, and I thought about the way Mark O'Connor and different people would invite him to play rhythm guitar on their records. I thought he was probably okay with that.

I figured that would be a pretty neat thing to do, to put his magic carpet ride under some of my tunes that might have saxophone solos, or get him to play with Victor Wooten and Future Man. We brought together Edgar Meyer and Paul McCandless from the band Oregon, and Tony as a rhythm player, but some soloing too. It's a special record, a very melody-oriented record for me. I wasn't looking for a shreddy kind of record. I was looking for different people to come and go, so he came and went. Maybe he's on four tracks.

I knew he liked the Flecktones and I thought, *You never know, maybe it would click and he'd want to come out and do some shows with us or something.* But it never happened. It was fun though and he did great.

There were also lots and lots of times where we all played on the same session, when we had all agreed to play for somebody. So I think if you add it up, there was quite a lot of interaction.

I do remember being in California when they were doing one of the *Bluegrass Album Band* projects.

Was this during the Leela era?

Yes. They lived in Corte Madera, because we'd stay at that motel there when we did stuff with him, the Corte Madera Best Western.

But when I first came, he had me come stay with him, when I came for Sam's benefit, and for the *Double Time* project. I slept in his extra room.

He turned me on to great coffee. He was into grinding coffee beans for each cup, and told me exactly how many seconds to grind it, before you let go of the grinder button. Everything he did had to be just so.

And then he had these speakers, I remember them. He'd play me music through those speakers, but it was jazz usually. There was some Dave Grusin stuff he really liked, the piano player. And there was classic Blue Note* jazz type stuff, and it sounded unbelievable on those speakers, it was just so killer.

He really didn't want to play a lot. He wanted to listen to music together and drink coffee and that kind of stuff. I kinda begged him to get his guitar out so we could practice the song we were gonna record. And then when he got it out and it went like real fast. He played it a few times, and I was like, "Yeah, that'll be fine. Yeah! Great!"

So in a way he was likely to get the guitar back in the case pretty quick, even back then. I don't know what that was about.

I know that the DGQ practiced a ton. You were there. You were

---

* Originally dedicated to recording traditional jazz and small group swing, the Blue Note label began to switch its attention to modern jazz in the late 1940s.

in that band.

We tried to get together to play five days a week. If we had one gig that week, we rehearsed four nights. If we had four gigs, we'd still rehearse on the fifth day.

Yeah. It paid off.

And he practiced all the time. The instrument was virtually never out of his hands.

Well, as time went on I think he didn't seem to want to do that. I suspect he had hand issues long before anybody knew about them, because I know he loved to play.

He was unable to pull certain things off at a certain point. There was a moment where the tempos weren't working well, he couldn't play fast solos anymore. Something had happened … and he was frustrated. It bugged him.

And Sam would say, "You can't just show up and not warm up and expect to be able to play like that." But I think there was something going on that he wasn't telling anybody, about his hands. That's why he begged off the *Bluegrass Sessions* tour. He said his hands were really hurting him. And that's the first time I ever knew that.*

And his driving himself solo from gig to gig was established at that point. He'd show up just in time to play, and peel out immediately after the gig. The suspicion was that Tony couldn't handle the idea of being on a tour bus with all of us. It was just too close. It was too exposed.

Do you remember the last time you played with Tony?

We played the night after Tony's IBMA Hall of Fame induction, on the big stage; he showed up for that. This is worth talking about.

He didn't practice with us, and nobody knew if he could play,

---

* Bluegrass Sessions was released in June, 1999.

and people suspected that he needed the money, so he might show up. But nobody really thought he was going to show up. It was hard to believe.

But then all of a sudden it was time to go on, and he appears on the side of that stage. It's a high stage, way up off the ground, with steep stairs to get up the scaffolding and to the stage.

And I'm standing there, I got my banjo, the whole band is there, and everyone has practiced, but he hasn't, and he says, "Hey man, what are we startin' with?

And I said, "I think we're doing 'Roll on Buddy.'"

And he said, "How fast? Kick it off and show me how we'll play it."

So I kicked it off, and he went, "Oh man, that's too fast. We can't do that."

And I was like, "Well, I don't know what to tell ya."

And then we're standing there for a few minutes, and he just started strumming his guitar. And it was like, "There it is! There's the sound." And I started rolling along with him.

He got in this groove and we started playing, very mid-tempo, but locked in. It sounded great.

And I was thinking, "Oh! There it is. I've missed this so much …" and then he stopped.

The set was a tough set for him. But he showed up, ya know. He showed up. We had a plan to let him play solo at a certain point so that he could … do his thing. But he played. And yeah, that was the last time.

I have that it was billed – this is the Red Hat Ampitheater – as Sam, Jerry, Béla, Alison Krauss, Del McCoury, and Mark Schatz. Is that your recollection?

I don't remember Alison coming out, though I could have that wrong. Maybe Del came out and sang something. That's possible, but Tony was billed, I believe.

He wasn't the Tony Rice we once knew. And the way he looked was crazy, like his body was being eaten away from within. He was so thin.

As odd as he'd been, and how distant and all that kind of stuff, after the show we all went back to the dressing room, and they had gotten us all dinner, and we sat there and ate a big meal and hung out. It was the old Tony, happy and convivial and very normal.

Here's another gig I remember, while I'm thinking of it.

We had these amazing gigs at the Birchmere, which were partly special because it was a place where you could hear yourself well. We did two nights there with Sam and Jerry, and I think one year it was Alison Krauss, and maybe another year it was Stuart Duncan.

The night before the gigs we met up at a Best Western somewhere, and had a rehearsal in a hotel room. It was one of these tiny hotel rooms, so small. There's two queen-sized beds in it, and this whole band is stuck in there, between the beds, and a couple of us are sitting on the beds, a couple of us standing in between, and Mark's got his bass, and Tony's got his guitar.

And as I remember it – this must have been the year Stuart was there, not the year Alison was there – we all took a hit of pot. And we played the music.

Say what you want about pot being good or bad for music. You know, sometimes you get high, and it's really fun. But then you listen back and you go, "Oh my God! It doesn't sound anything like I thought. I was having this amazing experience and now that I hear it, it was horrible."

So, say what you like, but we were all on exactly the same wavelength. And we took it to the moon. Everybody was playing their hearts out for hours in the room.

And then afterwards we all went to some steakhouse and had this huge, wonderful meal/hang together. It's probably one of my best memories of all. All of us being together in that group, because we just really were together. The gigs were spectacular. Yeah, some good memories.

It seemed like he ate a huge meal. He was always so thin that you never expected him to eat anything. But no, he chowed down. It seems to me he had a big steak.

Everybody had a really fun time time together. And we didn't have a gig that night. We'd rehearsed early enough that we could all go get a great dinner somewhere. And I'm sure we drank glasses of wine or whatever. It was a happy time.

I also remember him coming to my house, playing my guitar, and, ya know, kinda … smashing it up. Drunk, at some point.

I didn't say a word. He had my 1950 D-28, and he was scratching it up, gouging it…

Someone said, "Are you going to let him keep doing that?"

I said "Yeah."

Cosmetically, he tore up the guitar. And I was perfectly happy about it.

Yeah, I saw that period when Tony was drinking a lot. I didn't like it; I wasn't happy about it. But I wasn't in a position to judge. Probably when someone's older than you, from a generation before you,* you don't feel comfortable suggesting what they shouldn't do… If a younger musician who was talented had a problem I would be more likely to talk to them and try to help them.

I think Jerry Douglas was more of a kind of guy who had a peer relationship with Tony. He would advise him. They were pals.

---

* Tony is seven years older than Béla.

And Sam too, though there were some frustrations between the two of them sometimes.

Cuttin' Up with Sam & Tony

I remember one night. Ya know, Sam likes to cut up during the show. And he likes to roll up your pants leg while you're trying to play a hot solo. And it was fun. Tony ... well, he'd laugh about things but he was there to play the music. He was very dead-pan during the show.

So Sam got into that pants rolling thing with Tony, and we came off stage and Sam was furious because Tony didn't back him up with the humor that night. Everyone else could go there and go along. And Sam was really angry at Tony and let him know it. Ya know, hittin' it ... with high volume.

And Tony said, "Sam, if you keep talking like this, you're going to hurt my feelings."

And that defused the whole situation.

Tony had a way of dealing with Sam. He and Sam ... they were brothers. They loved each other so much. They'd been through a lot. They were there at the beginning, when neither of them were anybody, and they were there at the end. Along the way there were some brotherly disagreements, or frustrations, I would say.

I also saw times when Tony did things that Sam was correctly furious about or irritated about. But all of us who were there will always remember when Tony said that to Sam.

I remember Leela being very sweet. She was a photographer, right? Maybe he didn't think he deserved somebody like that. I don't know; I don't know what was between them. She wasn't really around much when I was at their house. But she seemed wonderful to me.

Yes, she was a wonderful gal, and Jerry said she was the best thing that ever happened to Tony.

Yeah. Sometimes somebody who's troubled doesn't think they deserve that. It seems like she tried to take care of him.

Will anyone ever come along and replace him?
They haven't so far. That was my problem with this album [*My Bluegrass Heart*].

Finally I needed to make the record, Tony wasn't going to come back, this was before he died. In fact my plan was to ask him to write the liner notes for it, because he wasn't able to play anymore.

I didn't want to make that kind of record without him. Even though I love playing with Bryan Sutton, there's just something about Tony. So I had to get over it and make some music without him. And when I did that I discovered, as you know, that other people have skills Tony didn't have.

All the guitarists on *My Bluegrass Heart* were very conscious of sitting in Tony's seat. And I would have loved for him to hear how everyone referenced him while being completely themselves. He would have been proud … I like to think.

But when you've played with the very best, and they're older than you, and they're a hero, it's hard to replace them with the new cats. The guy who came closest to him was Mark O'Connor, oddly enough, on guitar. I mean Mark played with that drive, he had the rhythm down, he played stunning solos. It was not a Tony imitation, but he had more of that quality than anyone I'd heard back then.

Again, I love Bryan, I love Cody Kilby, I love Billy Strings – he's like a primitive Doc Watson on psychedelics. They're really fun to play with. But they don't do what Tony did. They just don't.

Every once in a while you run into someone who has the rhythmic wherewithal to make the music dance. Critter Eldridge, to me, can make the music dance very well. He understands that element, although maybe some other elements are his number one thing. But he's got that. Cody Kilby comes pretty close to doing that.

Every once in a while you run into somebody who's got that. They'll have one thing or another. There are lots of guys who play all over the guitar, who are real good at being all over the guitar. And that's always cool. But they usually have a different language than Tony.

When you hear somebody who plays too much like Tony, it's a problem. You don't want them to play that much like Tony. And you've got the Tony clones, which there are quite a few of, and some of them are better at it than others.

I kind of wish Wyatt would step up and take over the mantle, because he'd probably be the closest thing. He's a great musician in his own right, and he's got the legacy and he's got the rhythm. I think he could play a wonderful role in the community. I think he knows how to drive a band like Tony did.

Tony had a jazz aesthetic. I also think he had some limitations as a jazz guitarist, and I think he knew it. For instance, do you know that 1981 live album *Friday Night in San Francisco,* that John McLaughlin did with Paco de Lucía and Al Dimeola … the three guitars?

Had you heard that after they fell out with Al Dimeola, they were auditioning other guitarists to be the third guitarist, because they didn't want to do it with Al anymore? And they asked Tony to audition, and he wouldn't do it. The honest truth is that those guys played with a speed that probably would have been beyond him, and he probably knew it. He would have brought something else to it that would have been pretty unbelievable in his rhythm. So many things he would have brought to it. I wish he would have done it and tried it at least.

I think that straight ahead jazz was not his thing. He played the chord changes, and he'd play through standards. He played busy, like a bluegrass musician, same problem I have when I play jazz … learning how to create space. He created a hybrid bluegrass-jazz form that was influenced from his years with the DGQ. It wasn't my favorite thing about him, honestly, being a bit of a jazz lover.

If you didn't know jazz and you were coming from bluegrass, you might be 100 percent blown away, but if you listen to Coltrane, and you listen to Miles Davis, and you listen to Chick Corea, and you listen to a lot this other stuff …

Some of his tastes were kinda smooth. He liked some pretty smooth-sounding stuff.

But on the other hand there are guys like Pat Martino. To me he's the Tony Rice of jazz, and maybe Tony is the Pat Martino of bluegrass, but Pat Martino had this very specific language that only he played on guitar. If you didn't really listen, you'd think it was repetitive, but the truth is he was constantly reinventing that language and he would do the same licks over and over in new ways.

You'd wait for Tony to do the Lester Flatt run at the end of the solo and land the thing. He might do the thing that he'd been developing for years, this one way to end a bluegrass solo, he'd do it over and over again. I'm sure you know the one I'm talking about where he'd start at the twelfth fret with a harmonic, and then he'd play the tenth fret *F*-chord, and he'd work his way down the neck, and then all of a sudden he'd hit this blinding Lester Flatt run, played after all this syncopation, harmonics and chord motion, and land this thing. And it would blow you away, every single time. It didn't matter how many times he did it.

He had this certain language that he played over and over again, and he got better and better at it. He learned this language that he created all over the guitar, and you loved to hear it. You would love to hear it.

To me Pat Martino was the same thing. You knew what he was going to do. You knew at some point he was going to play this three-note pattern for two minutes straight till the whole crowd was screaming. He would do it every night, one time. He would do these exact kinds of chromatic jazz, one-chord vamp things. Nobody else did them, and it was fabulous to listen to.

There were people who you could say were more advanced harmonically, or could do more kinds of different things, could play subtler, or whatever, than Tony. But he had a rhythmic intensity that nobody had. He was very aggressive rhythmically. Tony had rhythm. He didn't have the harmony that some guys had, but he had that same rhythmic intensity to what he played.

To finish up on that, on my years of playing with a lot of great jazz musicians: I always feel that I play one on TV, but I'm not a real one.

But with Chick Corea, his message to me was, "You can play anything you want, as long as you play it with a lot of confidence. Try it. Try anything. Play it like you mean it. Play a half step off. Do whatever you want. Play it like you mean it." And Tony always did that.

You talk about his drinking. Everyone knows he went through drinking periods. Could you see what caused the drinking?

No. I don't really think I knew him well enough. I just knew it couldn't be a good thing. And it was a beer thing usually when I was around him. A lot of beer. But it was always disappointing because it meant we weren't going to have a great jam.

Remember, I'm mostly in my twenties when I'm hanging around Tony. He was seven years older than me. That's enough to be another generation.

Have you heard how he died?

I'm not sure that I know the truth. I know that he was found and the coffee was going and the water was running maybe and he was on the ground.

For a while there – Peter Rowan and others reported this – he drove with one of his people from A.A., a sponsee, but Tony wouldn't let the guy drive. He did all the driving himself.

I've heard something along those lines. I knew there were times he had somebody with him. And he would pull up ten minutes before the hit and miss the sound check.

Yeah. Yeah. He just wanted to walk out and play and be gone. Not a happy guy.

The last ten or fifteen years were very painful for him, in his hands, in having had to give up the guitar, in losing his voice. I think they were very difficult years.

Well, what about the whole watch thing? He seemed to get a lot of pleasure out of that.

He was expert at repairing Accutron watches.

Yeah. Amazing. We are all wearing these Accutron Tony Rice T-shirts these days. A guy named Jake Schepps started making them. It's a T-shirt with the Accutron works and a guitar combined. And its kind of a secret code. Anybody who puts that on is a Tony Rice worshiper. You see them at the festivals. When we played the Tony Rice tribute show at Rocky Grass last year, a bunch of us were wearing them.

Flux* said that anytime you see someone wearing an Accutron watch, it's not because of Bulova, it's because of Tony.

Yeah, anybody in our scene. A lot of guitar players found that if you showed up with an Accutron watch Tony would let you in the door.

---

* Jerry Douglas's nickname

He was influential in more ways than just the guitar.

Yeah. And he was so smart. He was a very, very bright guy who knew a lot about a lot of things. He had the whole photography side of him too.

Anything else you can think of?

That's kinda what I got. I was hoping it would be worthwhile. I don't know if I have anything earth-shattering that was unknown, but just a lot of respect and pride to have gotten to make some special music with the guy.

I think about him all the time. I talk about him all the time, him and Chick Corea. I dedicated *My Bluegrass Heart* to both of them. In fact, the last time I communicated with Chick was Christmas Day, that same day that Tony was found. Chick didn't die until a couple of weeks later – I didn't even know he was that sick – but that was the last time he texted with me in a normal fashion, and then the second week of January he died. We lost a lot of people these last couple of years.

I remember Tony would say "I love you" a lot to his collaborators. I don't think he did that lightly. He got over the stigma at that time of saying "I love you" to people enough that he could say it easily to the people he wanted to.

So I got a few of those, and they were very meaningful for me.

Frank Poindexter is the Rice brothers' uncle on their mother's side, the brother of their mother, Louise. He's known Tony all his life, played music and recorded with him in his earliest days. And he was one of the very few to know Tee during his final, hermetic decade.

Frank is an outstanding dobro player. At 74, he is still on the road, pickin' and singin' with the band, Deeper Shade of Blue.

He's played the Grand Old Opry – that's a distinction right there – and with Vassar Clements, Dickie Betts of the Allman Brothers Band, all the Rice brothers, and on two movie soundtracks.

His tone on the resophonic guitar, or "reso" as the dobro is also known, is sweet, deep, smooth. In knowing how to caress a note, Frank's playing puts the cry in the high lonesome sound of bluegrass.

In my interview with him, Frank expressed much with few words, leaving much to be heard between them. Although the interview lasted only 38 minutes, it was revelatory.

It is difficult to communicate with text the pregnancy of a pause, the rhythm of a rephrasing, a catch in the throat, and above all, the heart, all evident in speech.

What I heard in Frank's voice was his love for Tony.

Frank Poindexter Speaks

Frank, how do you remember Tony Rice?

I remember Tony as a very close family member all my life. They[*] were living in California; I was in North Carolina. And when they came in about every other year, Tony said he had his hand on the door knob to get out of that car as soon as it pulled into our yard to see his Uncle Frank.

So, I've always been real close to Tony and we've had a very good loving relationship with each other. As far as being actively playing music, when Tony was 14 and I was 15, me and him and Larry and Herb and Ronnie, we played at this place in Crystal River Florida called the Wander Inn.[†] Herb used to call it the "Wander In and Stagger Out."

I lived in Safety Harbor but I would drive up to Dunnellon and Crystal River on the weekend. I'd spend the weekend with Tony and Larry and Herb, and we would play music. We had a great big kitty [jar] and we'd play just for the kitty, and that's how we got paid. So, come Saturday morning we'd be counting out a lot of single dollar bills.

Let me fast forward and tell you about when Tony moved in with my mom and dad, his grandparents.

---

[*] Herb, his wife, Louise, and the Rice brothers
[†] This was the "Wander Inn of Crystal River," a restaurant, Pure gas station, Western Union, and Greyhound Bus station, now Heritage Antiques, at 103 Northwest US Highway 19, Crystal River, FL 34428

W e were watching this local TV station out of Greensboro, North Carolina, [WUBC], and heard this guy Bobby Atkins.[28] They had a show called "Stone* and Atkins." And we recognized how good Bobby was on the banjo. He sounded like he had Scruggs down to a T.

And I said Tony, "We need to go up there and jam with him." So we took off and went to Greensboro and that TV station. They done all their shows live and when they came off we went in and said, "We want to know if we can jam with you."

He said, "You got your instruments with you?"

And we said, "Yeah."

So we got the dobro and the guitar in there and started jamming with them. And the next week we were on the show with them and then we started playing with Bobby Atkins and that's how the *1968 Session* record came to being.

1968 Session was an Old Homestead record [OHCS-126] that was put together from all the recording that [we did with] me and Tony and Bobbie Atkins and Rita and Shirley Williams, a couple of girls that done real good back up singing, good harmony.

We didn't even know we were doing a record at that time. Every time we'd get a little bit more money, we'd go in and buy some studio time. And Tony even dubbed the bass in on some of that stuff we were doing.

Later, about 1974 or 75,[†] Old Homestead released that on a vinyl LP. To this day it's still good quality. And no more instruments than we had: it was just a dobro, a guitar, a banjo, and a bass. We didn't have fiddle, we didn't have a mandolin. That record is still considered a good recording.

Tony's Passion

We were on our way back to the house one night after playing a

---

* Joe Stone, guitar, was dropped when Tony and Frank started playing gigs with Atkins, instead recording commercials at Crescent City Sound Studio.
† It seems to have been 1981. Atkins was also a Bluegrass Boy.

gig with Bobby and them, and I was contemplating how much passion Tony had for the guitar. That was his life. That guitar was his passion day in and day out. And on the way back to the house I came up with this question. I said, "Tony, what would you do if somebody locked you up in a room and you didn't have your guitar. What would you do?"

Immediately, without thinking, he said, "I would beg them to let me have some kind of stick that I could close my eyes and pretend that I'm holding that guitar."

Does that tell you the passion he had for that guitar?

Frank, what year was it that he moved in with you and your folks?

That was about 1967 or 1968.* Tony lived with several of our relatives. He lived with the Smiths, Hal† and his wife Joyce, for a while. Tony used to stay at Joyce's parents'. He also stayed some at my sisters' house, Nelva and Cecil. He would sleep over at Bobby Atkins' house. He stayed at a lot of places. We come from a family of 15 you know, there's 15 of us Poindexters.

At the time he was living with us he was heavy, heavy into Doc Watson. We had Doc's albums there at the house, those LPs. And Tony seemed to fall in love with Doc Watson. He played that stuff note for note. I mean you couldn't tell it wasn't Doc Watson you were listening to.

In 1970, we went to the festival at Camp Springs near Reidsville, North Carolina. Sam Bush and the Bluegrass Alliance band was there. Tony was in a jam with them, and the next thing I know he's saying, man, he's got the gig, he's gonna be leaving with them going to Kentucky.

I said "Well cool; I'm gonna get married."‡ I was in love at that

---

* Tony would have been 16 or 17 years old.
† Hal was Frank's brother.
‡ He married Pam in November, 1970.

time. And since that time we've stayed in touch with each other. We didn't miss many chances.

Tony's career took off, and I couldn't have been more proud of what he done.

The solo project that I did, on Mountain Fever, called *It's the Music*,* that's the last time that Tony, Larry, Ronnie, and Wyatt, all four, was in a studio at the same time.

I've got good memories of that. My sister Louise, Tony's mother, was there at the studio with us. We had the best time. That was in 2004.

That record never was on a major label up until this last year, and Mountain Fever released it on a digital recording. Matter of fact Joey Black, he's incorporating it into the playlist of XM radio,† which I'm very proud of.

Why did Tony move out of his home to live with you guys and other people?

It was a broken home, Bill. It was a broken home.

You know, Herb, Tony's dad, was an alcoholic. And Louise, my sister, she had to leave numerous times. She couldn't be in the same house with Herb because Herb would get drunk, and he would cuss and he would go all wild.

It was a broken home. That's the answer for you right there.

That's why Tony and Larry, Ronnie and Wyatt, they've had a very rough growing up period with their dad. I mean, he's been an alcoholic the whole time. … They all left the house that they were staying in. Louise left.

And then he had a cigarette to catch the bed on fire, caught the house on fire. It didn't go up in flames so to speak, but the smoke inhalation and the heat in the house was how we lost Herb. That's how he died.

He just was an alcoholic, and he just went crazy and when he got

* Released May 10, 2022
† A SiriusXM show called "Bluegrass Junction" with Joey Black

like that, they all got out. They got out of the house and just left.

It's very sad to think, cause when Herb was sober, you couldn't meet a nicer man. He was a very educated man. He was talented. He held a good job, he made good money. He put bread and butter on the table for the family.

He bought instruments for them. He bought Tony a D-28. He bought Larry that mandolin, that Gibson mandolin. It's in the Hall of Fame* right now by the way … that mandolin. That's another story right there, in itself. I won't get off course, I know we're talking about Tony mainly.

There weren't many people who were in touch with Tony the last 10 to 15 years of his life when he became a bit of a hermit. Were you in touch with him then, Frank?

I was, I was. But only on Tony's timetable. Tony would call me when it was on Tony's brain. I could call him and leave a message and I wouldn't hear from him for a while, and then I would hear from him.

Tony's Depression & Frank's Antidote

Tony got very depressed. He got depressed that he couldn't play because of his pain in that right hand, and he was very very depressed, and he talked about …

I said, "Tony, all you have to do is sit back, sit back and just smile and say 'Yeah I did that; I did that.'"

He was talking about going to colleges and workshops, oral workshops with people, and talking about the music, music theory and stuff like that. He talked about that quite a bit, but he never did get that going.

And then he said, "You know, this doctor in Danville, Virginia, has offered to do surgery on my hand, and he said it won't cost me a dime."

---

* The Bluegrass Music Hall of Fame & Museum in Owensboro, KY,

And I said "Man, that's good news, Tony. God, that's great."
But he never pursued it; he never let that happen.

Tony's passion in those Accutron watches kept him alive for several years. You know he always loved those Accutron Spaceview watches. It got to the point he said, "I don't know how these damn things work, but I'm gonna find out."

Tony, he got with this retired Bulova engineer, and he learned everything he could from him. He got the microscope, he got the tools, he got the parts. Tony could take one down to the whole chassis, every single part. He rebuilt hundreds, I'm talking literally hundreds of watches, for himself and other musicians and fans and friends.

He would go and do a session for somebody and rather than get paid in cash he'd say, "You got any old Accutrons?"

They gave him Accutron watches for parts and stuff like that. Tony is a perfectionist when it comes to doing something like that.

I've got a box full of Accutrons that he rebuilt for me, and Ronnie's got watches he's rebuilt for him.

We've traded and swapped. I've got this solid gold Accutron he fell in love with, and so we did some swapping.

He had this purple flight case that he was getting ready to replace, and I said, "I'll trade you for a stainless Accutron and your old case."

He said, "It's a deal."

I ended up with Tony's purple flight case and I got a D-18 in it.

Tony had anxiety; he took medications for his anxiety.
Tony knew his health was going down, but he wouldn't
… he wouldn't

... he wouldn't

... he wouldn't get the attention that he should have got.

Do you know Pam had moved out of the house, I don't know, two, three, or four years prior to Tony passing away? Tony was by himself in the house when he passed away.

Do you think watchmaking made him happy?

Yes. He loved that.

Now, I think that towards the end, it was taking his toll on him. I think when his health was going down, He was slowing it down a little bit on the watchmaking. But I think the watchmaking took up what would have been a void in his life. I think the watchmaking really helped him for a few years. I think so.

He said, "I don't know how these damned things work, but I'm going to find out." And boy he did; he found out all right.

Do you remember the last time you spoke with Tony?

I do. I was telling Tony about this liquid vitamin that I take called Liquid Power.

He made himself show some interest in it, but it was ...

And I asked him, I said, "Tony, can I pick you up and we can go down to the lake,* just me and you, nobody else? And we can own a boat and we just ride?"

He said, "Frank I want to do that more than anything in the world. But it's not the right time." He said "It's not the right time right now." He was so depressed.

I said. "Tony please let me know when we can do it."

But I knew, I could tell he wasn't gonna leave the house. I mean, he had friends that would come and bring his groceries that he ordered and leave them out on the grill in the carport. Tony would leave the money out there. Tony wouldn't even come out. He

---

* Lake Tillery, Norwood, N.C. where Frank and his wife have a home and boat

Tony and Frank Poindexter at The Moon
Tallahassee, Florida, 2005
– Photo by Laurie Hillis

didn't want nobody to even see it, Bill.

Very, very sad. Dang. I mean the whole thing is just so sad, it breaks your heart. Looking back at it, Tony wasn't reaching out for the help that he needed. He knew he was going down, and he allowed that to happen. What other conclusion can I come up with? I mean he wouldn't get the help. He wouldn't have that surgery. He wouldn't go out and get a good healthy meal.

So basically he just gave up. Very sad. But he sure left a legacy behind that nobody else could ever replace.

Tony was a giant in the world of bluegrass.

Oh yeah. He was. There was many people that would imitate him, but there's nobody on this earth could ever do what Tony could do musically.

He was our hero.

And his voice! Tony's voice in bluegrass was the best voice I've ever heard sing a song in my life. No one could do it better than Tony … his voice. I mean, he had class. He had that class. Wow, what a voice he had! He was the absolute best.

Whatever I told you,
it's coming from the heart,
it's the truth,
and
there's nothing else I can do.

The Rice Family – July, 1960
L to R: Ron, Tony (9 years old), Dorothy, Larry & Herb Rice
with Herb's Gibson Style A-4 mandolin
11949 205th Street, Artesia (now Lakewood) California
– photo courtesy of Ron Rice

CD album cover of Native American, *Rounder 0248*
– Photo by Mark Farris

" ... Tony had a real fascination for John Wilkes Booth, down to the point where I think he owned one of Booth's jackets, one of his coats. And he had a copy of it made and he wore it on his Native American *album cover." - JERRY DOUGLAS*

JWB & Native American

Tony's interest in John Wilkes Booth (JWB) – the actor and President Abraham Lincoln's assassin – was with him when we played together in the 1970s. Books about Booth were lying around his Corte Madera apartment.

Ron Rice wrote, "I do know he was a JWB nut. I have seen a couple of photos of him wearing a jacket similar to the one on the [*Native American*] album cover standing beside or leaning against JWB's gravestone."

About these graveside photos, Pamela Hodges Rice wrote, "Bill, there was one in the bedroom before the flood in Crystal River. Tony had it level with the bed for some reason. On the side next to the blue bathroom. It most likely washed away when the swirling of returning water went back out to sea. I'm sure there were negatives of it, but I'm not sure if they survived."

In his interview, Jerry Douglas suggested that Tony was "more interested in the lifestyle of Booth and the way he always dressed better than the other actors." Ron Rice made the point that Tony was more interested in Booth the actor. I'm sure they're both right.

On the other hand, Tony commissioned Mary Chapin Carpenter to write a song about Booth he recorded on *Native American,* one she titled "John Wilkes Booth."

The song calls Booth "a patriot."[29]

Mary wrote it, but apparently Tony had asked her for a rewrite of the song. Jerry said, "I remember Chapin coming into the studio with the finished version of it because Tony asked her to rewrite something and then she came in and we cut the song."

I don't know what the rewrite was about ... the music, the lyrics, both ... ? I tried to make contact with Mary Chapin Carpenter about this, but never heard back.

Mark Schatz spoke of that album: "I think the name of [that recording, *Native American*] has to do with his perception of what native American was. I don't think it was native American like the people who lived here before [Columbus arrived]. I think it was kind of 'us,' ... white people. There might have been a little resentment of immigrants, newcomers. I heard Tony make some disparaging comments from time to time, about someone working at the 7-11, 'can't hardly speak English,' or something."

Norman Blake told Schatz that Tony referred to his Lincoln Continental as "Wilkes Booth."

Kari Estrin, Tony's agent and manager for about five years, wrote this: "I didn't really want to engage in looking at John Wilkes Booth as a patriot – so I guess his views are in Chapin's song.

"I thought it odd about his fascination with Booth, he would talk about him and about some aspect of his life, and kept reading more about him ... but didn't delve into his thing with Booth. But it occupied Tony's time – and yes, that coat was worn on *Native American*. He was quite proud of that!"

Tony played with Mountain Heart from approximately 2009 to 2012. Josh Shilling, one of his band mates, wrote me, "He did mention John Wilkes Booth occasionally. I remember that he would sometimes sign the end of his text messages as "JWB." I feel like I remember him leaving voice mails that way as well. 'Hey baby, call me back ... it's John Wilkes Booth.' ... I've always heard stories about Tony and JWB."

So Tony was interested in Booth from at least Jerry's time with him, in 1974, to at least 2012 and Mountain Heart. Forty years, possibly more.

Finally, in the *Native American* liner notes, Tony wrote, "Speaking on behalf of Mary Chapin as well as myself, neither of us could condone such a criminal act as the one committed by John Wilkes Booth."

L ooking at these stories from people who were with Tony at various points in his life, it appears he was widely read and well informed about John Wilkes Booth. His interest spanned at least four decades. He was a student of a man we think of as Lincoln's assassin, but whom Tony thought of as … as what?

A person can become enraptured by a historic figure, and Tony's long obsession with Booth was that. What initiated his fascination – Booth as assassin, actor, dapper dresser, or yet something else – is unclear.

What is clear to me is that Tony's interest in JWB was another layer of his layered being.

Photo found on Herb Rice's living room wall after the fire of November 20, 1983
– courtesy of Ron Rice

Tony's Father, Herb Rice

On December 1, 1983, Tony told me his father, Herb Rice, had died in a fire at his home eleven days before. "He got in bed with a lit cigarette, the bed caught fire, and he was too loaded to get out," he said.

"I'm so sorry to hear this, Tony. My heart goes out to you and your family."

"Aw, that ol' man was nothing but a mean ol' drunk." He spat it out.

Tony had three brothers, Larry, Ron and Wyatt. Larry died in 2006. Ron, born in 1955, and Wyatt, in 1965, carry on the Rice Brotherhood. Ron told me this story in greater detail.

"When Dad died, he … the part about the cigarette is true. He passed out drunk in the bed with the cigarette. And then he woke up and he went into the kitchen after that, and he passed out sitting in the kitchen chair with his head on the kitchen table. In the meantime the mattress is on fire and smoldering. So he wakes up and he realizes what's happening. Then he goes into his bedroom, and beside his bed is his guitar. And that's when he's overcome by the poisonous fumes that were being put off by the mattress burning.

"Dad was a violent drunk, no doubt about that. I don't know why, other than it goes back to that automobile accident in 1959. The night before Thanksgiving in 1959,* we were in a pretty bad

---

* This must have been November 25, 1959; Tony would have been 8½ years old.

car accident. Up until that point, my dad, he never drank. Just a typical father with kids who moved to California and was making a living for his family.

"Up until the accident [dad] was like Ward Cleaver.* The typical 1950's dad wanting to raise a family.

"Until that point, Dad never touched a drop. That was his pre-drinking, pre-alcoholism [era], I guess. The perfect dad, he spent time with his kids. Larry and Tony had baseball uniforms when they were in Little League, [and Dad] attended games. He took us to L.A. Dodgers games. He was that kind of person.

"But he was like Jekyll and Hyde whenever he would start drinking. Totally different.

"My wife tried to explain to me the difference about that. My dad came from probably a half-Indian background. You know the old myth about firewater and Indians. My wife explained to me that over in Europe, when they first discovered wine and alcohol, that the violence it would activate in a person, trigger in a person, was eventually bred out of Europeans' genes.

"But that was strictly Europeans, and it never reached [American Indians]. Indians, back in the day, didn't do all that stuff. I mean they didn't drink wine or anything like that so when they did get alcohol in their system, the violence and the anger would get triggered at a certain stage. I don't know if that makes any sense to you or not.

"So that could've been what triggered something in him, or it could've been the accident. I know Larry had a bad drinking problem. Tony had had one.

"Tony looked at Dad like he didn't want to become that, so I don't recall Tony ever drinking. When they played in Kentucky with J.D. Crowe in the lounge, when they'd go on break, Larry and Crowe and them guys would have a drink. Tony would either have

---

* Ward Cleaver Jr. is a fictional character in the TV sitcom *Leave It to Beaver*.

a cup of coffee or a Coke.

"When Tony started his drinking stage I've got no idea. Maybe some point in California when he moved out there."

It may have been when he and Leela broke up.

"It could've been. Before then he was not against it but he just didn't care for it."

I don't remember Tony from my period with him (1976-1979) as a drinker.

"Never was. I never saw the drinking side of Tony until he left California and moved to Florida. And I was totally surprised by that, because I always seen him as not anti-drink, but it just didn't interest him at all. And it seemed to me like he didn't want to be like his father."

Do you have good memories of playing music with your dad?

"Oh yeah, yeah. I mean, all the time. When we were kids he had a tape recorder and he'd tape us at different stages. And all of those times he was totally sober. During the week he was pretty much the ideal dad.

"The music come along, and we'd be playing music on Friday or Saturday night, or Sunday afternoon – though not so much on Sundays because he had to go to work on Monday. But a lot of times, it was a trip to the liquor store on the way home on a Friday afternoon. Up until that point he really encouraged Larry and Tony musically.

"Dad and I were probably the closest out of the four of us.[*] But him and Tony and Larry, they were different. He really encouraged them to play music. He was constantly bragging on them, what good musicians they were and that they were going to make

---

[*] I believe Ron meant that he, like his dad, did not play music for a living. The other Rice brothers, Tony, Larry and Wyatt, did.

a career out of being a musician.

"He totally encouraged that. As a matter of fact, what father, back in the '60s, working as a welder in an air conditioning shop, would go to McCabe's* and buy his son an F-5 mandolin?

"He did the same thing with Tony. He bought him a D-18 guitar, and then after we moved to Florida, he bought him a D-28 from some music store in Ocala.

"I've got recordings of some of this stuff that dates back to 1959 [when Tony was eight]. I've got one recording of Tony singing "Battle of New Orleans." He was seven or eight or right in between there. His guitar playing wasn't all that great. Dad would play that Joseph style,† the bar chord style of guitar. And Dad is playing that style of guitar, and Tony is singing "Battle of New Orleans" and he totally nails it. At the time I was four. He recorded all of this.

"Ten years later here comes Wyatt, and Wyatt is not in school yet, but he's getting pretty close to being either in preschool or first grade. We were living in Virginia, down by Hampton and Newport News, and Dad saw that Wyatt was interested in playing music, so he went and searched all over the place for a guitar that Wyatt could put his fingers around and make a G chord or whatever chords they make on a guitar. And a regular dreadnought-sized guitar, he couldn't find one. So he found a small Gibson guitar, about the size of one that Willie Nelson would play, at a pawn shop.

"It had a small enough neck that Wyatt could get his fingers around there and make chords and stuff like that, and he recorded us each and started Wyatt out playing "Little Brown Jug." Three days later Wyatt is playing "Little Brown Jug" and making G-runs between chord changes and stuff."

---

* This is McCabe's Guitar Shop in Santa Monica, California.
† Ron is referring to Joseph Strader, his grand-uncle, who listened to Django Reinhardt and was influenced by Django's chording style.

Herb's Love of Animals

"Squirrels in the yard or birds in the yard, he would have them eating out of his hand within hours of seeing them. I mean, squirrels would come right up to him. He would hold his hand out and the birds would just fly and land on his hand. He was that kind of person. Animals loved him for some reason or another.

"He was great with animals. He could teach a dog the difference between a squeaky newspaper and a squeaky bone. He could train animals to do unheard-of things that normal people couldn't get them to do. He was pretty good at stuff like that. He could train dogs and small wildlife.

"He loved to fish. Dad and I went fishing numerous times, had really great fishing trips.

"As long as he wasn't drinking he was a really cool guy. Not a great musician, but he could play. He was a good tenor singer in the Golden State Boys,[30] and in the other group he migrated off to, Tom and Herb (The Bluegrass Ramblers). They were actually a pretty good band.

The Accident

"It was a pretty bad accident, in Artesia,* California. It was at the corner of Pioneer Boulevard and Del Amo Boulevard. I was just four. Pretty young.

"The state failed to maintain a stop sign at the intersection. It was a truck route, and when trucks would come by and try to make the turn at the intersection, they would cut it short and take the stop sign down. So, that was the cause of the whole accident.

"A lot of people were hurt. There were 12 people and 11 of them wound up hospitalized. Tony was the only one [who escaped serious injury].

---

* Now it's called Lakewood.

"[My father] was injured; everybody was injured. Tony had a few scratches, but other than that, everybody else was pretty seriously injured and wound up in the hospital.

"After the accident, that's when my dad started drinking, and then, the violence started showing up. His injury was a fairly serious concussion. So I don't know if that was the cause of the violence and the drinking or what.

"You remember the old cars that had a rearview mirror on the dashboard? Well, Dad had a car with a fold-down armrest in the middle of the back seat. They would fold it down and that's where I would sit. During the accident, I flew from that seat over the front seat, hit that rearview mirror and it ripped my head open, practically from front to back. I had a compound fracture on my left leg and wound up in the hospital in traction for six weeks.

"Everybody in the car flew out of the car, and the car was upside down in the middle of this intersection. The people who hit us, they were in a '57 Plymouth station wagon. There were six people in their car too, and they all wound up in the hospital.

"Larry was hurt. He wound up in the hospital. I'm not sure what happened with him, not a whole lot. He was like in and out of the hospital.

"My grandmother on my dad's side, she wound up with two broken arms. The car landed on Mom, on her back, and she had some serious back issues, and Dad had a concussion.

"All I remember is that they were putting this mask over me, putting me to sleep, and the ether smell was awful. I don't care if I never smell that stuff again. That was their way of anesthesiology I guess, back in the day.

"We had just come back from shopping. Dad liked to go to the grocery store on Friday and get all the groceries to last a week. You make one trip a week to the grocery store and that was it. Since it was Thanksgiving, they went shopping the night before.

"As a matter of fact that's the last thing I heard from Tony, the Thanksgiving before he passed.

"He called me up on the eve of Thanksgiving, and said, 'Man, this is like …' – you know how he was a technical with dates and stuff – he said, ' … this is like the sixty-first year of that accident that we had in California.'

"Those were the last words I heard from him, other than like 'Hey man, I'll talk to you later.'"*

In compiling the anthology of men's writings, *Heart of a Man,*[31] I read many stories by sons about their fathers. Dad's love can be tough love, sometimes forging a distant, contentious relationship.

As starters, Herb was not always supportive of Tee's pickin'. Tony told me his dad said to him, "You'll never be no Clarence White."

Ouch!

Ron and Wyatt Rice interpret Herb's saying this as having been spoken in haste, because Herb encouraged his sons' musicianship, bought them instruments.

Steve Swan and Tony lived together in Corte Madera for a year, 1984 to 1985, following Tee and Leela's breakup. Steve had broken from his girlfriend in the summer of 1984. "I moved up to the 'saddest home in Marin County' after a drama-filled breakup of my own. We were brothers in romantic misery after that."

Alcohol

Some of who Tony was can plausibly be linked to his alcoholic dad. Children of an alcoholic parent can lead wildly differing lives, I understand. But it seems they all dip from a pool of common behaviors.[32]

A son of an alcoholic can have relationship problems. Tony's

---

* November 26, 2020 was Thanksgiving day. So Tony's last words Ron heard him speak on the phone were likely on November 25, 2020. Within a month, Tony had passed.

three marriages,[33] his liaisons with women on the road, and rumors of children he may have fathered – we'll look at that on the next page – possibly point to that.

Depression and anxiety can dog the child of an alcoholic, and they certainly dogged Tony, as Jerry Douglas and Frank Poindexter said. The child of an alcoholic does not express his feelings openly,[34] studies show. He can be emotionally contained. Almost all the folks I spoke with said some form of, I didn't really know him or, He was hard to get close to.

Needing to exert control over one's life is the trait of the child of an alcoholic, and one of Tony's, as we've read

Children of alcoholics can abuse alcohol and other drugs; we've heard these stories about Tony and are soon to hear more.

Tony was sober during the DGQ era. He toked, but not that much or that often. Coffee and cigarettes were Tony's drugs of choice. He sometimes seemed like a sad guy, inside a shell, but I think that, like Sam's era with him, the DGQ era (at least during my tenure), spent playing music he *loved,* was apparently, at least on the outside, a happy one for Tony. Inside, I can't say what was going on for him. As Peter Rowan said during his interview, "We will never know what his personal life was really like."

Finally, the need to succeed follows many children of alcoholic parents. Tony's flourishing on the guitar was urged on by his drive to succeed *and* to show his dad he was wrong about never being a Clarence White. The latter is something not all guys on the I'll-show-Dad quest achieve. *Way to go, Tony!*

I'm sure Tee loved his father, in spite of what he said to me about Herb when he passed. A son trying to exceed Dad's expectations of him is a son showing Dad his love.

Herb Rice was a mandolinist, and introduced the four Rice brothers to bluegrass. But having to support a wife and four sons, he was a welder for a living, and apparently an excellent one. Tony always spoke highly of Herb's welding skills, and Frank Poindexter alluded to them as well.

I find an analog to this in comedian Steve Martin's remembrance of his father, Glenn Martin, published in the *The New Yorker*.[35] Steve's dad had always wanted to be in show business, but sold real estate to earn a living for his family. Steve remembers him as "angry," and "critical of [Steve's] show-business accomplishments."

On his deathbed, as he said his final goodbyes to his family, Glenn said to Steve, "You did everything I wanted to do."

Steve replied, "I did it because of you."

It's possible to imagine Tony did it because of Herb.

Stories & Rumors

Liaisons happen on the road and children can result, sometimes to the ignorance (or denial) of the dad. I heard a few stories that Tony fathered children by various women. We've heard Jerry Douglas's story of a man who threatened to shoot Tony on stage over fathering a child with his sister.

There's another story of Tony having fathered a daughter, replete with a photo of him holding her as a child, a 2021 email from her as a grown woman, plus a photo of her standing next to her mom at her college graduation. People who could be skeptical about this story, believe it.

Both these stories have credence. In his memoir, *Crossing Bridges,* Mark O'Connor alludes to the brother who threatened to shoot Tony on stage, writing that Tony "refused to attempt another DGQ performance in the South after that." The daughter story from Ron is also credible.

– photographer unknown

Repeating other rumors I've heard of children Tony allegedly fathered, stories without evidence, would not be right.

Finally, I believe that all children who are consensually conceived are heaven-blessed. Something tells me Tony felt that way too.

The Rice Boys
L to R: Tony, Herb holding Wyatt, Ron, Larry
Safety Harbor or Clearwater, Florida, summer of 1965
– photographer unknown

Last Chorus

S ad stories are hard to tell. Worse, they're usually long.
This one is both. It's based on stories that were related to me, but also on the North Carolina Medical Examiner's Report and Toxicology Report on Tony's death.

I've debated this section in my head, questioned including it, and if I included it, then what should I include ... and exclude?

What do we learn from it?
Certain information is learned.

Will some resent it?
I hope not. It's just more sides of the Tony we love, truthful and factual.

Moreover, the North Carolina Medical Examiner's Report is a publicly available document. I'm trying to gently sum it up, minus the graphics of the original, and with the addition of some informative narrative.

If you want to shield yourself from the medical facts of Tony's end, please skip this chapter. On the other hand, I've heard from some of Tony's friends who expressed needing closure on his passing, who wanted to know how he died, so they could put him to rest in their thoughts and hearts. I hope this chapter brings resolution for them.

Tony became hermetic in his last years, as we've read. Ron Rice said, "I went by several times; Wyatt did too. He would come out into the yard, but that would be about it. We couldn't go in the house. Then it got to the point he wouldn't even come out in the yard."

Peter Rowan told me a story that echoes Ron's.

"The last conversation I had with Tony, I was in Florida driving up to North Carolina, and I called him and said, 'I'm gonna be right by your driveway, can I come by and say hi?'

"He said, 'I'd love to see you but I can't see anybody. I just can't.'

"And it was like, 'All right, Brother.' I mean, what was I going to say?"

Tony's Hobbies

Tony had a few hobbies over the years. I mentioned he was a student of John Wilkes Booth. He went through an era of photography and became quite good. I remember him, with a tripod-mounted Canon F-1,* clicking off a remote shutter shot of a red rose in a clear glass vase in front of a black velvet backdrop, meticulously set up, precisely controlled and executed. All very Tony.

Repairing Accutron watches was Tee's last hobby, if that's the word for something one becomes expert at, renowned in the Accutron community.

Ron Rice said, "If you wanted a watch repaired, if you wanted to drop off some parts for him or something, he'd say, 'Put it in the mailbox and I'll pick it up later.' It got pretty bad.

"Tony had this fear that if he left his home, somebody was going to come in and take his guitar. So, he never would leave his home."

Certainly "The Antique" is a valuable instrument, and as Golda Meir said to Henry Kissinger, "Even paranoids have enemies." So I understand Tee's wanting to guard it vigorously. But not leaving the house because he feared the instrument would be stolen was

---

* At one point, Ron Rice said, Tony owned eleven Canon F-1 bodies.

far more obsessively vigilant than Tony was back in my day.

Medical Examiner's Report

The North Carolina Department of Health and Human Services, publicly available "Report of Investigation by Medical Examiner," an eight-page document, and the "Toxicology Report," two pages, detail Tony's passing.

Tony was last seen alive by a family member on December 21, 2020. His death was discovered on the evening of December 25, 2020, by his stepdaughter, India. Although he might have died on that day, the report says he "died in his home on an unknown date." On Christmas night, December 25, India knocked on Tony's door. When he didn't answer, she forced it open and found him kneeling in front of the kitchen sink, water running. The sleeve on his right arm was caught on a cabinet in an upright position while his body was crouched on the ground.

Ricky Skaggs announced that Tony Rice passed "sometime during Christmas morning while making his coffee." As Jerry pointed out, it was unlikely Tony was making coffee in the morning. Though he might have been brewing java – it is already part of Tony's myth – the Medical Examiner's Report does not mention it, and checks the "Unknown" box next to Tee's "Activity" at his time of passing.

Non-Work Related: *(See Examples Below)*

FATAL INJURY OR ILLNESS: Activity_____ ■Unknown

Type of place_home_____ Specific location kitchen_____

Examples-Activity: Running, lifting hay bales, eating, typing letter, driving commercial truck, sleeping, bathing, watching television, fight, etc.

Type of place: House, apartment, trailer, school, jail, bar or tavern, hotel, restaurant, store, street, hospital, farm, highway, factory, etc.

Specific location: Bathroom, assembly line, kitchen, front yard, office, parking lot, emergency room, roadside, ambulance, etc.

Discrepancies

The Medical Examiner's Report estimates he was 6 feet, 2 inches, and weighed 100 pounds. He was wearing a "green button-up shirt, flannel pants ... black socks and brown shoes." He wore "one yellow metal ring with blue stone,* three yellow metal rings, one yellow metal ring with a clear stone, one yellow metal brace-let, one white metal watch," the last almost certainly his Bulova Accutron 214 Chapter Ring Spaceview. To paraphrase the lyrics of Jimmy Driftwood's "Tennessee Stud," the report states that the color of the sun in his eyes was green.

But the "Examination of Body" reports he measured only 5 feet, 10 inches and weighed in at 105 pounds. He had a mustache, and a spare, grey-brown beard. His brown hair was long and matted. The color of the sun in his eyes was brown.

Though there are discrepancies between these reports, remark-ably in the color of his eyes and in his stature, they both report extremely low weight for a man of Tony's height. A man of 5 feet 10 inches, for a proper Body Mass Index, should weigh 132 to 167 pounds,[36] not 105. Tony was 27 to 62 pounds underweight.

As Peter Rowan said, "Though a thin guy, he went from a fairly strong, robust physique to 98 pounds and yellow, sallow skin[†] by the time we finished playing. I remember our last gig. I was shocked. He was like a skeleton."

In a space titled, "Probable Cause Of Death," the two boxes, "Probable Cause Of Death" and "Manner Of Death," are both checked "Pending." This indicates that a supplemental death cer-tificate will be issued once testing is completed.[37]

But to the right of it is a box labeled, "This Section 'OCME RE-VIEW ONLY'"[‡] and is footnoted with, "Information in this block supersedes that contained in space at left." Here, inked in, as the

---

* This is likely Tony's star sapphire ring that be bought at a Lexington jewelry store when he was 20 or 21. Ron Rice accompanied him.
† Sallow skin is indicative of anemia. The Medical Examiner's Report states that Tony received a blood transfusion to treat this in 2019.
‡ "OCME" stands for "Office of the Chief Medical Examiner"

only "Due To," is "Atherosclerotic cardiovascular disease."[38] That's cholesterol plaque buildup in arterial walls, obstructing blood flow, a.k.a. heart disease. This seems to be this page's conclusion, although a "pending" one, waiting completion of testing.

I thought that a diagnosis of this disease would require an autopsy, but as we see, next to "AUTOPSY," the "None" box is checked. I found no follow-up to the "pending" probable cause of death as heart disease.

AUTOPSY: ■ None   □ M.E. Authorized   □ Non-M.E./Private-Facility Name:_____

BLOOD SAMPLE : Mailed by: □ME after External □Pathologist after Autopsy ■Reason not obtained: ^{obtained at second external by OCME}

IF CLINICAL ALCOHOL PERFORMED, RESULT:_____ Where:_____

PROBABLE CAUSE OF DEATH: ▣ Pending

	This Section "OCME REVIEW ONLY"	SDC
1._____	1. _Atherosclerotic cardiovascular_	None
DUE TO	DUE TO _____ _disease_	AL
2._____	2.	Dictated
DUE TO	DUE TO	(COG)
3._____	3.	
DUE TO	DUE TO	
4._____	4.	

CONTRIBUTING CONDITIONS

CONTRIBUTING CONDITIONS

MANNER OF DEATH:

MANNER OF DEATH:
□ Natural □ Accident □ Homicide □ Suicide ■ Pending

(Natural) Accident   Homicide   Suicide   Undetermined

Reviewer: _____   Date: 04/01/2021

Information in this block supersedes that contained in space at left.

Ron Rice said, "He wouldn't even let Wyatt or me in his house, just because of shame. His house was run down. His wife … [had] moved out. They hadn't been living together in two or three years if not longer than that. They were both pretty much hoarders. Tony at one point had nine dogs, I think.

The Medical Examiner's Report states:

"Decedent was crouched on his knees on the floor, [in front of the kitchen sink] face down. His right arm was hung on the handle of the cabinet above him. … There were three canines and a small bird in the house. The house was unkempt with immeasurable amounts of items in every room. There was little room to move through the house and some rooms were not able to be occupied due to the amounts of items collected and stored in the room. The house was not sanitary due to immense amounts of animal feces throughout the house. The decedent has a medical history of substance addiction to hydrocodone and Xanax. … Decedent was sent to the N.C. Office of the Chief Medical Examiner for follow-up on suspicion of overdose …. "

The house being in disarray, the dogs' mess, Tony's hair being matted – unexpected for a guy so fastidious in appearance – his weighing 105 pounds … Where do these point? To Tony's not caring about himself or how he lived? To the painkiller cocktail, as we're about to read, found in his blood? I don't know.

Mark Schatz said, "Anybody who saw him two or three years before he died, he looked like he could roll over and be gone, he was so frail. In a way, he lasted much longer than many expected. He was depressed. People who are depressed will stop eating. It'll kill you, a really serious depression will."

The Toxicology Report

All who knew Tony, as we've read, believed that he had twelve-stepped away from drinking in the mid-1980s. But the toxicology report from the Office of the North Carolina Chief Medical Examiner showed Tony had ten substances in the blood they drew from him including ethanol, the active ingredient in alcohol.

The others were benzodiazepines, caffeine, chlorpheniramine, dextromethorphan, nicotine, opiates/opioids, Xanax (as Alprazolam), hydrocodone, and hydromorphone.[39]

Ethanol

The level of ethanol found in Tony's blood was low, 20 mg/dL. A Blood Alcohol Concentration (BAC) of 10-50 mg/dL can cause "mild euphoria, decreased inhibitions, diminished attention & judgment."[40] And 20 mg/dL is in the *low* end of that 10-50 range.

But the BAC in the blood of a cadaver can change with time. It can go either higher or lower than the true BAC at death.[41] Further, we don't know the date and time of Tony's passing, so we don't know how long it was before they took the blood sample from him. And finally, we don't know if the alcohol that Tony had apparently ingested, represented the only nip he'd sipped in decades; if he'd been long off the wagon; or something in between. (I'm on "the only nip in decades" side.)

Three Other Drugs

But we know this: three of the substances present in Tony's blood should not be mixed with alcohol:

1. Xanax, a sedative to treat anxiety and panic disorder, is a "controlled substance."[42] Combined with alcohol, it can slow breathing and possibly lead to death;

2. Dextromethorphan is a narcotic related to opium. One should avoid taking it and drinking alcohol which can increase the side effects of dextromethorphan: severe dizziness, anxiety, restless feeling, nervousness, seizures/convulsions, confusion, hallucinations, or slow, shallow breathing; and

3. Hydromorphone, a narcotic, can cause respiratory distress and death when combined with alcohol.

This is an excerpt from the Medical Examiner's Report:

Other diagnoses: severe anemia for which he had a transfusion in 2019 and was non-compliant with supplements prescribed by his physician, anxiety, depression for which he refused to take an anti-depressant, and B12 deficiency. No foul play suspected.
Decedent could not be positively identified due to changes in his facial appearance. Decedent was sent to the NC Office of the Chief Medical Examiner for follow-up on suspicion of overdose and to be identified.

I saw Tony and Peter Rowan backstage after their set at the 2005 Hardly Strictly Bluegrass Festival in San Francisco's Golden Gate Park. I don't know how many gigs followed this one in their tour, but when Tony walked off stage, he got on the phone to cancel them all.

Though he had been scoring his tortoise picks to make them rougher and easier to hang on to, he could no longer take the pain of holding the pick and flatpicking. For Tee to cancel a tour was a farther bridge than I'd ever seen him cross, by a far piece.

To my eyes, both the Medical Examiner's report and the toxicology report point to the same place: the heart and body of a man buried under an avalanche of pain.

Who Was Tony Rice?

Tony was a complex personality who drove himself hard. We're the beneficiaries of that, in the least through his recorded oeuvre; Tony loved making albums and played on over 250.[43] Folks who never saw him in concert will be able to hear his recordings, watch videos of him, be inspired by him, for as long as long lasts.

I know a few musicians in their golden years who are abandoning their instruments because their hands, like Tony's, have deserted them, or some debilitating illness is visiting them. Most are floundering in high seas: What do I do now? Who am I if not a picker?

So for Tony, who had the instrument in his hands constantly, it must have been deeply challenging and depressing to put it down. His Uncle Frank says it's what drove Tony's depression.

The only issue that makes abandoning an instrument easier is the debilitating pain that arrives with playing it, a simple one to take a pass on. It demonstrates the approach-avoidance conflict: you want to approach something – pick guitar – but you also want to avoid the pain associated with playing.

Was watch repair a replacement for flat picking the Dreadnought?
I think it was. As Frank Poindexter pointed out, Tony loved it. Clearly he became deeply immersed it, again, as only Tony obsessively could. Though he likely used his fingertips more than his

hands, the hand supports everything the fingers do, and there's no getting away from arthritic hands. The ache can be masked, narcotized for the length of a chorus, but it always reappears, a minor-key refrain of debilitation, pain, and frustration.

There was a certain respect, maybe obeisance, that folks showed Tony when in his company. This was the Eric Clapton of the Dreadnought. You listened to him picking on stage because he had so much to say on the Herringbone, so you listened to what he had to say in the dressing room or at the party. Tee was deified – still is – by many folks in the bluegrass community.

I played music with him, hit the road with him and five other guys (including the DGQ's manager, Craig Miller), shared trains, planes and automobiles for hundreds of miles at a clip, and re-hearsed with him sometimes five days a week. I can separate Tony the Guitar God from Tony the guy. It was the guy whom I toured with, hung with, got to know. The pickers I spoke with for this book had the same relationship with him.

That Tony, the one I knew, was a hugely fun person to be with. With a music group, he could be the spirit of the gig and the life of the after-gig party or meal, joking, sometimes storytelling. He "did" characters from his life, famously a Louisville cab driver, Bill Snowden. Bill had lived five lives, including one as a boxer.

Snowden had a crooked mustache. Tony would put a curved in-dex finger to his lip, at an angle, and quote some famous Bill-ism in a broad Kentucky accent – "Now Tahny," he'd say, "Ah killed a man in da ring one tahm," – to laughter all around for Tony's way of telling it.

Peter Rowan said, "As a person, he was very charming and funny, one of the funniest people I ever met. He did this whole take on meeting Bill Monroe, with Monroe talking about me,

Grisman, Sam Bush, and Earth Opera [Peter's band]. Tony's sense of humor was very outrageous at that time – it was more ironic later on – but he was so funny. He could imitate everybody, anybody. He kept us in stitches the whole time."

Yes, Tee was a fun hang, a crackup, an entertaining guy who brought smiles to all faces nearby.

But the path of a young musician – practicing alone while everyone else is socializing, playing music while everyone else is on the dance floor – can forge an introverted, under-socialized being. Tony could be sociable at times, but turned inward at others. As Mark Schatz pointed out, there was a certain formality to his persona, a somewhat stiff, formal posture.

He hid his pain. The night he crashed on my sofa, he hinted at what was bringing him down. But he was unwilling talk about it.

Peter Rowan remarked, "Tony had a life, but he was very secretive about his life. He was the classic artist. Tony put everything into his music. He was an extremely sensitive and perceptive and simpatico musician, in my experience. As a musician, as a person, he was a sweet guy, but he was carrying a lot of weight, a lot of weight. We will never know what his personal life was really like."

Tony had genuine warmth and could be both kind and generous. Absolutely.

He always greeted me effusively and made me feel welcome with a big hug. I never saw him turn down a fan's request for an autograph.

On a few occasions, both in France and here, I saw him coach guitarists who approached him for help, folks he felt merited his time and teaching. I never saw money exchanged. Recognizing young talent and giving lessons to deserving youngsters has a long tradition among working musicians, one Tee joined in.

Well done, Tony.

He could be a deeply caring soul, as Mark Schatz noted.

Peter Rowan spoke of Tee's relationship to fiddler Vassar Clements:

"Tony told me he met Vassar because his parents and Vassar's parents were friends in Florida. Vassar was an older kid. [He was 23 years older.] And he said they would picnic on the beach and go net fishing. None of this is public knowledge, but Tony told me as a kid, their parents would go out to the beach at Little River or somewhere down there on the coast, and they would net-fish and have a barbecue on the beach and that Vassar was just an older guy who Tony really looked up to.

"Through the years, Vassar and Tony had a companionship. It was always very special when Vassar showed up at one of our shows and we played together.

"Tony was in Vassar's hospital room almost daily while Vassar was dying. He was at the hospital in Nashville for months because Vassar was an older brother to Tony."

Yes, Tony could be all these things: caring, warm, generous, hilarious, but sometimes lonely, sad.

But as Jerry Douglas said, "He was totally in charge of what was going on with him."

The contributors to Tony's complexity – his music upbringing, his father, the A-type drive to play guitar and show his dad wrong, his father's death, his three brothers, the loss of one, Larry, in 2006, his divorce from Kate, his heartbreaking divorce from Leela, the drinking, the painkillers, the teachers, the language licks and Golden Ears, the rigidity, his exposure to jazz and other music genres, the JWB preoccupation, the Rush Limbaugh tie, the adulation, his emotions and innate drive, his hands, how he heard, thought and played, the exact location of his brain between his ears and hands, and yes, the coffee – conspired to make him his era's titan of the flat-picked Dreadnought, of bluegrass guitar.

Some of the complexities of Tony's life – over-caffeinated, over-drinking, not eating right, picking the guitar so hard he hurt himself, refusing operations, the drugs of his later life and death – conspired against his productivity, helped bring his music career to a premature end. But we applaud his pedal-to-the-metal drive, the life he led as a wholly dedicated artist, the world master of his practice.

He was sharply focused on music, a sharper dresser, a blast to hang with, a crackup, funny as hell, but centered in his drive to arts excellence and always married to his guitar, giving his all to the guitar, the guitar always in his hands, health, longevity, and other issues be damned.

In the world of American music he was a hunger artist suffering for his art form, acoustic music, which lived inside a country music era long plugged in and amplified. His tangible reward was incommensurate with his artistry and acclaim, something he obliquely expressed to me at a gig.

The DGQ opened for Crosby, Stills & Nash one evening. Backstage, a number of Crosby and Stills' fine instruments were perched on stands: Martin Dreadnoughts and Triple-Aughts, a D'Angelico New Yorker, a Gibson J-200, and a few electrics.

Tony looked at the lineup of pristine instruments, tuned, buffed, and staged carefully on stands by a roadie, and remarked, "They should be mine."

If Tony had switched to playing electric guitar in country music, and brought along his golden country voice, he'd have been a million-seller. But he was true to his acoustic, bluegrass guitar self.

Like he said when he took a pass on playing a French luthier's custom cherry red, solid-body electric guitar: "It's a different instrument."

Rice Family Band, circa 1966
At the Wander Inn, Crystal River, Florida
L to R: Larry, Tony, Walter Poindexter, Ron, Herb,
and unknown man with a tummy-ache.
– photo courtesy of Ron Rice

What Made Tony Run?

These are the turnstiles of Tony's life, as I came to see them:

1. Being born to a musical family – his dad playing mando, encouraging his boys in music, buying them instruments – was pivotal to Tony's discovering and loving bluegrass.

2. The family car accident in 1959, when Tee was 8½, changed Tony's life and the relationship he had with his dad, who, as Ron Rice said, became "a violent drunk." Tony quit high school after 11th grade and left home at age 16.

3. Playing with J.D. Crowe from 1971 to 1975 at the Red Slipper Lounge, along with Ricky Skaggs, Jerry Douglas, and Bobby Slone, was the beginning of Tony's bluegrass stardom. He was 20.

4. Marrying Kate Freeman in 1972, his first marriage, at age 21, was good for Tony. As Jerry said, Tony liked being married, and Kate *adored* him. At the DGQ's first gig, I remember her sitting next to the stage, looking up at him starry-eyed.

5. Playing with the original DGQ album band in 1976, when he was 25, was pivotal in Tony's listening to more music outside bluegrass, and in his contribution to the creation of a genre debuted by that album, one he termed "New Acoustic Music."

6. Tony's divorce from Kate, in 1979, was a turning point for him. It's possible that his drinking, slow at first, started around then.

7. Marrying Leela, the great love of his life, on September 28, 1980, was the beginning of a good era for Tee. Jerry Douglas said she was "the best thing that ever happened to Tony." He cut *Mar*

West, Still Inside, and the first three *The Bluegrass Album* recordings during this period. He formed the first "Tony Rice Unit."

8. In the Spring of 1984, Leela left their home. It put Tony in a depression, and witnessed the dawning of a harder drinking era. (When he roomed with Steve Swan, from August 1984 to '85, he was drinking every day, Steve said.) On May 1, 1986, their divorce was finalized.

9. After baching it for a few years, Tony, 38, married his longtime friend, Pamela Hodges, on August 8, 1989, his third and last marriage. In photos from that time, they look happy together and very much in love, as they did the last time I saw them in 1991.

10. The loss of his ability to play without pain, so much that it affected his career, appeared to begin when Tony was 54, at the 2005 Hardly Strictly Bluegrass fester, when he canceled the rest of the Rowan & Rice tour.

He might have canceled gigs previously, I don't know, and by 1999 Béla was aware of Tee's hand pain. In a 2007 interview with guitarist Scott Nygaard, Tony said, "My playing was more straight-ahead up until about ten or fifteen years ago. Then I started to get arthritis in my right hand, and now I have tendinitis real bad in my left hand – over ten years or so."[44] So, his hand problems started as early as 1992.

He played out after the 2005 Hardly Strictly fester, including a 2007 tour with Alison Krauss and Union Station. He didn't sing except for one time. Jerry said, "I remember him leaning into the mic once and singing a low harmony part on a song just for a few words. The crowd went wild."

And he played on a 2009 Mountain Heart tour. But he wasn't singing and, though he pushed himself to some sustained choruses, some of them Tony-brilliant, he doesn't sound as sure or fleet-fingered as before, and he wasn't flogging the instrument as he had ... but he was still remarkable.

Some albums he'd played on were released post-2005, but both his gigging and recording output flagged. Tony's last released album, in 2011, *Hartford Rice Clements,* with Vassar Clements and banjo player John Hartford, was recorded 23 years earlier, in 1988.[45]

The last recording of him singing that I can find, done in 1997, is of Tom Waits' "Pony," with Jon Carroll playing piano. If you only visit one link from this book, this is it. You may want to sit down first.[46]

11. His last time playing out, September 27, 2013, at IBMA, was the end of an era for him and for us, his fans. He played the Red Hat Theater with Sam Bush, Jerry Douglas, Béla Fleck, Mark Schatz, Del McCoury, and Jason Carter.

To me, the Rowan *&* Rice tour cancellation signaled the beginning of Tony's last waltz. When he started canceling tours because he could no longer play, did he also start withdrawing from seeing people, stop taking care of himself and eating right?

Tony changed in a few ways during his life. (Yes, we all do.) He went from someone who always had the guitar in his hands, whether watching TV or eating dinner, as Doyle Lawson said, to someone who'd rather talk and drink coffee than unlatch the case and play, as Béla Fleck commented.

His aversion to driving with the band grew with time. In my era, the quintet piled into our Mercury station wagon and rode shoulder to shoulder for hundreds of miles at a stretch. No problem for Tony that I ever heard. He loved to drive, but didn't drive himself to the gig back then (unless it was local), not that I recall.

And certainly his weight loss was another change. He went from a healthfully trim figure, to looking haggard and older than his years. When I played with him he was lean, but not overly thin. He ended up, as Peter Rowan suggested, looking "like a skeleton."

As to his guitar: I saw him leave it inside the house when we went out for a bite to eat, for instance. He was watchful over "The Antique," but he could leave it at home.

Uncashed checks lying around? … Never.

Cluttered home? … Nope.

Whatever these were symptoms of – paranoia, depression, drug use, anxiety? – they weren't presenting when I knew him. I saw him as sometimes sad, sometimes shelled up, but not paranoid.

He was drug-enjoying, but not drug-abusing, except for cigarettes.

Competitive? Yes.

Anxious? Well, in retrospect … maybe so.

How Does This Add Up To Tony?

Tony's being was music-centric. His dedication to music – playing guitar, singing, recording, producing, concertizing, listening, learning – was his entire focus.

He loved playing guitar – *loved* it – and devoted himself to it because he cherished the thrill all pickers know: playing a note or chord, feeling the instrument vibrate your hands and body, hearing the sound permeate your ears … a consuming rush of delight. Tony loved that thrill more than almost everyone else. He *had* to hear the sound of his instrument in his ears, more than you and I, just as he practiced more than you and I.

Was this intense love affair with the guitar an escape from something, or a going to something?

When you're in the zone with your instrument, your consciousness is all sound, a cloud you float in. For Tony, this was its own pleasure but, also an escape. As he said to Mark Schatz, "While you're listening to really good music, you can't feel pain at the same time." Tony listened to really good music all day long.

As I heard stories from folks who knew him, I felt that if Tee succumbed to bad business advice, let his career follow his gigs, or failed to promote his albums, it was to get that over with and get back to playing. If he floated on the winds that blew him around instead of trying to redirect them, he'd have more time to play guitar.

Did he register somewhere on the Asperger's spectrum?

I'm no psychologist, but if this is true, then to the extent that it is, maybe it helps us see a swath of Tony's behaviors, from his fixations on language licks and John Wilkes Booth to his fixation on the guitar, as pieces of a larger jigsaw. It puts these behaviors in a named box with known dimensions, one we can grasp.

Jerry's saying Tony was "starting to have some … mental problems," is a side of Tony no one else phrased that way. His saying that Tony suffered anxiety from being at the apex of a music mountain was another unique observation.

Was Tee "obsessed" with the guitar?

Yes, in the best way possible. And while we're here, what's wrong with obsession? We should all be so dedicated to our art. Duke Ellington famously never took vacations. Someone asked him the reason, and he replied in effect, Why would I want to get away from what I love most? So it was with Tee and his guitar. It's possible that when the Clarence White Martin went boating in its Leaf case, it was the longest Tee, as an adult, had been without a guitar in his hands, well, until his hands started deserting him.

Was Tony a genius?

If Tony was a genius, it stemmed from inordinately long hours with his instrument – discovering the guitar, loving the guitar, experimenting with the guitar, shaking new sounds from the guitar, showing Dad he could best Clarence on the guitar – a genius born of dedication and perspiration, plus a measure of pain and pain avoidance, from which great art can spring.

His "concept" – the sum of his approach to picking, tone production, rhythms, touch, time, dynamics, phrasing, comping, and soloing – was a quantum leap beyond what was being done in bluegrass guitar. He was the most virtuosic musician I ever worked with. Playing ensemble with him at close quarters, having your ears filled with his exultation of notes, was thrilling. The drama he produced with an acoustic guitar could be heart-pumping.

For a while, every guitarist I played with after the DGQ suffered in comparison to Tony:

Does this guy put on a set of fresh strings before each gig?

Does he re-tune after each number?

What capo does he use, and how does he use it?

How are his ears, his hands, his time, his picking?

Most important, how does he open his case?

I'm trying to recalibrate, adjust my attitude. As Dizzy Gillespie said, "Anyone who blows is outta sight."

Tony played so hard, he wrecked his hands. The pain was crippling. As Mark Schatz stated, Tony was a "tortured artist," flayed by the demons of his hand pain, his dad's alcoholism, his divorce from Leela, his anxieties, his bouts with drinking and later with drugs, and his having to say goodbye to the guitar.

Ron Rice remarked, "A couple of years after his last gig he played, I asked him over a phone conversation if he ever picked up the guitar and played. His response was he picked it up and played a few minutes daily but I'm not sure how long that lasted."

As I heard more about his late life, I sensed a downward slide into increasing pain and plain ol' bad health. His last decade – a long time – must have been agonizing, witness the anti-pain drugs found in him when he passed. So, I was glad to hear Frank Poindexter say Tee found contentment in watch repair.

As Schatz pointed out, it was amazing Tony lived as long as he did. His last years are an elegy to soldiering on through end-game pain and bodily dissolution.

Last Story

The myth says that legendary bluegrass musician Tony Rice passed on Christmas Day at his North Carolina home while making coffee. Songs will sing he died of a busted heart.

My story is that Anthony David Rice died alone on December 23, 2020, around 6 p.m., less than an hour after sunset.

Tony has woken groggily, dressed, put on his specs, switched on the heater – it's 29° in nearby Greensboro – and is shuffling toward the kitchen, weak on his feet.

He stumbles to the sink, gropes for the faucet, turns it on hard. His eyesight fades to black, his head spins, his knees buckle and he collapses, fumbling for the countertop as he falls. It slips his grip and he sinks to the floor, the cuff of his shirtsleeve hooked on the base cabinet handle.

Tony slumps to his knees as in prayer, head bowed, his right hand pointing to the heavens.

Jerry Douglas with Tony at his last gig, at IBMA, September 27, 2013

– photo by Todd Gunsher

Last Bar

I asked Ron Rice, "What can you tell me about your brother Tony that we haven't read or heard about?"

He said, "He could work on automobiles. He was very mechanical; a lotta people never realized that. I mean, he could pull a carburetor off of an automobile, overhaul it, and put it back together. He could do a lotta serious mechanical work. I don't think a lotta people knew about it.

"He loved fishing. Him and I fished a lot when we were kids and even in our adult life we did a lot of fishing down in Florida."

Casting for large mouth bass on the Withlacoochee River
Near Dunnellon, Florida, early 1980s
– Photo by Ron Rice

In Memoriam: Tony Rice

Tony didn't have a recording studio in his home, a record company, or website. He didn't dance the social-media shuffle. Outside of a few hobbies that evolved over the years, he put all of himself into music, especially the guitar.

In his IBMA Hall of Fame acceptance speech, Tony said he wanted to express himself poetically through music. In doing that, he gave his hands to the Dreadnought and his voice to bluegrass.

Tony –

It was an honor
and a thrill
to pick with you.
My heartfelt thanks for all your lessons.

Music is
who you were,
how you lived,
&
how we remember you.

You left a large mark, Brother.
Well done.

Rest in
Music
&
Peace.

– Wild Bill

Afterword

In assembling this book, I learned about Tony. Everyone I spoke with was insightful about the guy, though I'm not sure if any, myself included, knew him all. As I said coming in, out of respect for the privacy of Tony and his family, I omitted a number of stories I heard about him. At least one, as Ron Rice quipped, was "*beyond* West Virginia."

We each spin our own takes and speak our own truths in the stories we tell. This is what we heard in these narratives: the truths of the individual speakers, their personal beliefs.

There were a number of Tony's sides that many of the folks who picked with him touched on. They knew the whoosh of being swept into Tony's groove as he kicked off a tune, how it felt to play time and changes with him, his magic carpet under your feet.

They all said Tony was a very funny guy, a crackup, a blast to hang with. They saw his sharp smarts.

They also saw his sadness, knew that something was up, but could not always name it or its cause.

Tony's musician friends understood the pressures he was under and the anxieties he suffered. They all felt his love, expressed many ways, and his big hugs, but they also felt his distance. They all knew unanswered phone calls, texts, emails.

Many witnessed Tony's refusal of help, or failure to ask for help; they said he allowed his decline to take place. Others said he was strong-willed, and captained his winter's passage; he lived both his life and his life's decline in full control, they said.

My most memorable story about Tony, because it is one of the most telling, is Béla's:

> "I remember one night. Ya know, Sam likes to cut up during the show. And he likes to roll up your pants leg while you're trying to play a hot solo. And it was fun. Tony … well, he'd laugh about things but he was there to play the music. He was very deadpanned during the show.
>
> "So Sam got into that pants rolling thing with Tony, and we came off stage and Sam was furious because Tony didn't back him up with the humor that night. Everyone else could go there and go along. And Sam was really angry at Tony and let him know it. Ya know, hittin' it, uh … with high volume.
>
> "And Tony said, 'Sam, if you keep talking like this, you're going to hurt my feelings.'
>
> "And that diffused the whole situation."

Béla's story shows us Tony's focused, businesslike, I've-come-to-pick attitude; his independence (in not going along with Sam's hijinks); his alertness to the personal dynamics of the situation; his understanding and love of his brother, Sam; and his knowing the words to defuse the whole situation.

The Clarence White Martin – "the guitar" as Jerry called it; "The Antique" as Tony dubbed it, also known by its Martin serial number, "58957" – has a robust life of its own. I ran into *many* people who have researched, written, blogged, and yarned about this guitar. A book titled, *The Legend of 58957,* would be thick with intertwining stories of this heralded instrument whose value is beyond worth. On the other hand, I hope this is clear: it's *not* about the guitar. As Sam said, Tony could pull good tone out of *any* guitar. In fact, ol' 58957, plagued lifelong by high action, was a difficult instrument to play.

There's a long gap in its provenance. Who bought it from Kinney Music in Huntington, West Virginia, after Martin (presumably) returned it to Kinney from their repair shop? When was it sold and to whom, who did the freehand woodwork on the rosette, and what trail did it travel to Clarence's hands in late-1950s Los Angeles, 2,300 miles away?

There are a large number of folks who played music with Tony whom I could have spoken with. But when I finished interviewing his uncle, Frank Poindexter, who knew Tony his entire life, I felt I'd completed a circle that began with my call to Sam Bush. Every interviewee suggested others for me to get in touch with, but with Frank's phone call, I felt I'd come home.

Tony Rice was a major force in bluegrass, arguably as influential as Bill Monroe. His playing defined modern bluegrass guitar and in turn the modern bluegrass group; it will echo for generations in bluegrass and new acoustic music bands.

Tales of Tony Rice – this Big Man with his Big Guitar – will circulate in the international bluegrass community for as long as bluegrass is heard. I hope these stories, by musicians who danced with him in space and time, join them.

Appendix

Tony & Leela's Marriage License

ATTORNEY OR PARTY WITHOUT ATTORNEY (Name and Address):

LEELA SUH SATYENDRA-RICE   TELEPHONE NO. 415-456-4079
P.O. BOX 823
KENTFIELD, CA 94914

ATTORNEY FOR (Name): IN PRO PER

SUPERIOR COURT OF CALIFORNIA, COUNTY OF MARIN

STREET ADDRESS:
MAILING ADDRESS: P. O. BOX E
CITY AND ZIP CODE: SAN RAFAEL, CA 94913-3904
BRANCH NAME:

MARRIAGE OF:
PETITIONER: LEELA SUH SATYENDRA-RICE

RESPONDENT: ANTHONY D. RICE

FILED

DEC 19 1985

HOWARD HANSON
MARIN COUNTY CLERK
BY _L. Ryan_
DEPUTY

JUDGMENT

[X] Dissolution   [ ] Legal Separation   [ ] Nullity

[ ] Status Only
[ ] Reserving Jurisdiction Over Termination of Marital Status
Date Marital Status Ends: ~~April 27, 1986~~ 5-1-86

CASE NUMBER: 125333

1. This proceeding was heard as follows: [X] default or uncontested [XX] by declaration under Civil Code § 4511 [ ] contested
   a. Date: DEC 19 1985   Dept. or Div.: 2   Rm.:
   b. Judge (name): BEVERLY B. SAVITT   [ ] Temporary judge
   c. [ ] Petitioner present in court   [ ] Attorney present in court (name):
   d. [ ] Respondent present in court   [ ] Attorney present in court (name):
   e. [ ] Claimant present in court (name):   [ ] Attorney present in court (name):
2. The court acquired jurisdiction of the respondent on (date): ~~October 26, 1985~~ ~~December 1, 1985~~ OCTOBER 21, 1985
   [X] Respondent was served with process. [ ] Respondent appeared.
3. THE COURT ORDERS, GOOD CAUSE APPEARING:
   a. [X] Judgment of dissolution be entered. Marital status is terminated and the parties are restored to the status of unmarried persons
      (1) [X] on the following date (specify): ~~April 27, 1986~~ 5-1-86
      (2) [ ] on a date to be determined on noticed motion of either party.
   b. [ ] Judgment of legal separation be entered.
   c. [ ] Judgment of nullity be entered and the parties are declared to be unmarried persons on the ground of
      (specify):
4. THE COURT FURTHER ORDERS:
   a. Jurisdiction is reserved to make other and further orders necessary to carry out this judgment.
   b. [X] Wife's former name be restored (specify): LEELA SUH SATYENDRA
   c. [ ] This judgment shall be entered nunc pro tunc as of (date):
   d. [ ] Jurisdiction is reserved over all other issues and all present orders remain in effect except as provided below.
   e. [ ] Other (specify):

Date: DEC 19 1985

► _Beverly Savitt_
(JUDGE OF SUPERIOR COURT)   ma

5. Total number of pages attached: -0-   [ ] Signature follows last attachment.

— NOTICE —

1. Please review your will, insurance policies, retirement benefit plans, and other matters you may want to change in view of the dissolution or annulment of your marriage. Ending your marriage may automatically change a disposition made by your will to your former spouse.
2. A debt or obligation may be assigned to one party as part of the division of property and debts, but if that party does not pay the debt or obligation, the creditor may be able to collect from the other party.
3. If you fail to pay any court ordered child support, an assignment of your wages will be obtained without further notice to you.

Form Adopted by Rule 1287
Judicial Council of California
1287 (Rev. July 1, 1984)

JUDGMENT
(Family Law)

Civil Code Section 4514
3110-84-79

Leela & Tony's Dissolution Judgment

Endnotes & QR Codes

I've placed a QR code following some of the music video websites found in these endnotes. Scanning a QR code with a smartphone will take your device's browser to the website associated with it. By the time you read this book, the nature or existence of QR codes may have changed, the websites they link to may no longer exist, have moved, or be loaded with malware. So, scan at your own risk. If you find an inoperative QR code, let me know by going to Vineyardspress.com and clicking on Contact.

1 … as the David Grisman Quintet is known. My first gig with Tony and what I'm calling, and has been called, the original David Grisman Quintet (which made the original DGQ album, with Todd Phillips on second mandolin, Daryl Anger on fiddle, David Grisman on lead mando, and me on string bass), was, I believe, on July 27, 1976 at the Great American Music Hall. The last was with the second iteration in a string of "unoriginal" DGQs, I'll jokingly call them (with Todd subbed out on mandolin), on May 5, 1979, in Lawrence, Kansas. I also played the "David Grisman Quintet Alumni Summit" at the Great American Music Hall on October 20, 1991.

2 Some question my spelling of his nickname as "Tee." They see it as "T." He took a business card from his wallet one day, signed it "Tee" and handed it to me. It may be that Tony's spelling changed over the years from "T" to "Tee" and not impossibly, back to "T".

3 en.wikipedia.org/wiki/Tony_Rice discography

4 Dolly renders a poignant "The Cruel War" as Tony accompanies her: https://www.youtube.com/watch?v=MnGgIyKNuOQ

5 The Red Slipper Lounge, in Lexington's Holiday Inn North, featured bluegrass six nights a week from 1968 to 1974. Veterans of that gig included J.D., who led the band, Tony, Red Allen, Jim Hatton, Ricky Skaggs, Jerry Douglas, Sam Bush, Larry Rice, Larry and Bobby Slone, Doyle Lawson, and four drummers at various times, Jim Hatton, Donny Combs, Jimmy Klugh, and Denny Woods. Tony started with J.D. on Labor Day, 1971, and continued to Labor Day, 1975, by which time the band had moved to the Sheraton Inn, just east of Lexington.

6 Crowe on the Banjo by Marty Godby. University of Illinois Press. Urbana. 2011. Pages 126-127

7 Bluegrass Unlimited, March 2021, 55

8 https://www.craftinamerica.org/artist/joan-baez#jp-carousel-8318

9 American Exodus: The Dust Bowl Migration and Okie Culture in California by James N. Gregory. Oxford University Press. New York. 1989

10 "Detour" by Patti Page https://www.youtube.com/watch?v=LNrDHaFcP2Y

11 Sam renders "Molly & Tenbrooks" https://www.youtube.com/watch?v=qJ1Rv64Mn6I

12 J.D. plays "Train 45" at https://www.youtube.com/watch?v=iXSZuKBtT2k

13 In a subsequent email, Sam said Tony couldn't see red, which is called protanopia. This website displays a colorful tableau as seen with normal vision and with protanopia. Point your browser to https://www.colourblindawareness.org/colour-blindness/types-of-colour-blindness/

14 See this performance of "Old Train" at https://www.youtube.com/

watch?v=YjwmKZ7D4Zg\

15 https://en.wikipedia.org/wiki/Jerry_Douglas

16 Known by its Rounder Records Catalogue number, "Rounder 0044," this landmark bluegrass album was state of the art. https://en.wikipedia.org/wiki/J._D._Crowe_%26_The_New_South

17 https://en.wikipedia.org/wiki/Ulnar_nerve

18 https://www.lyrics.com/lyric/1054274/Tony+Rice/John+Wilkes+Booth

19 You can listen to "Never Meant to Be" at https://www.youtube.com/watch?v=KSswjJ3m22g

20 https://simplecirc.com/bluegrass-unlimited/item/4717/tony-rice-feature

21 Tony's IBMA acceptance speech begins around 18 minutes in. https://www.youtube.com/watch?v=ZBzGDa5DAjE

22 Bluegrass Unlimited, March 2021, page 57

23 https://santacruzguitar.com/tony-rice

24 Tony plays "Shenandoah" and "Danny Boy" at the 2000 Grey Fox Festival

https://www.youtube.com/watch?v=J5UXCJopX6Y

25 Bluegrass Unlimited, November 2023, pg 27

26 Tony sings "Freeborn Man"
https://www.youtube.com/watch?v=RyCPwqRujd4

27 Tony Sings "John Hardy Was a Desperate Little Man"
https://www.youtube.com/watch?v=gNTeWVo16E4 or https://bit.ly/3AvUegX

28 https://bluegrasstoday.com/bobby-atkins-passes/

29 "John Wilkes Booth Lyrics." Lyrics.com. STANDS4 LLC, 2023.
Web. 9 Nov. 2023. <https://www.lyrics.com/lyric/1054274/Tony+Rice/
John+Wilkes+Booth>.

30 The Golden State Boys included, at various points between 1960 and
1964, Herb Rice, Hal Poindexter, Leon Poindexter, Floyd Poindexter [Ron
Rice does not recall his uncle Floyd being a member of the Golden State
Boys], Lee Casteen, Walter Poindexter, Don Parmley, Tom Kuehl, Bil-
ly Ray Lathum, Red Ashley, Scott Hambly, Harry Kniss, Skip Conover,
Bobby Slone, Vern Gosdin, Rex Gosdin, Steve Stephenson, Del Mc-
Coury, Billy Baker, Roland White, Larry Rice, Bob Warford, Eric White,
Chris Hillman, and Dennis Morse. https://www.facebook.com/media/
set/?set=a.243702452376486&type=3&comment_id=1517441781669207

31 https://heartofaman.net/

32 https://americanaddictioncenters.org/alcoholism-treatment/children

33 Only 5.3% of Americans have married three or more times. https://www.

washingtonpost.com/news/wonk/wp/2015/09/03/that-kentucky-clerk-isnt-alone-millions-of-americans-have-been-married-three-times-or-more/

34 https://americanaddictioncenters.org/alcoholism-treatment/children

35 https://archives.newyorker.com/newyorker/2002-06-17/flipbook/084/

36 https://www.cancer.org/healthy/cancer-causes/diet-physical-activity/body-wseight-and-cancer-risk/adult-bmi.html

37 https://www.ocme.dhhs.nc.gov/faq/OCME-FAQ-Pamphlet.pdf

38 https://www.webmd.com/heart-disease/what-is-atherosclerosis

39 1. Ethanol – a psychoactive drug, a recreational drug, and the active ingredient in alcoholic drinks; 2. Benzodiazepines – a class of psychoactive drugs that affect how the brain works and causes changes in mood, awareness, thoughts, feelings, or behavior; 3. Caffeine; 4. Chlorpheniramine – an antihistamine, it can treat hay fever, allergies, and cold symptoms; 5. Dextromethorphan – DXM is a narcotic related to opium that suppresses an area in your brain that causes you to cough; 6. Nicotine – a naturally produced alkaloid widely used recreationally as a stimulant and for relieving anxiety; 7. Opiates/Opioids – They may be prescribed for pain relief, anesthesia, cough suppression, diarrhea suppression, and for treatment of opiate/opioid use disorder. Both opiates and opioids may also be used illicitly by people with a substance use disorder; 8. Alprazolam – a.k.a Xanax, is a sedative. It can treat anxiety and panic disorder and is a controlled substance. It can cause paranoid or suicidal ideation and impair memory, judgment, and coordination; 9. Hydrocodone – an opioid used to treat pain and as a cough suppressant; and 10. Hydromorphone – a narcotic and controlled substance that can treat moderate to severe pain and carries high risk for addiction and dependence.

40 http://www.clinlabnavigator.com/alcohol-ethanol-ethyl-alcohol.html

41 https://pubmed.ncbi.nlm.nih.gov/16782292/

42 Controlled substances are drugs that are subject to strict government control because they may cause addiction or be misused. https://www.addictiongroup.org/resources/faq/controlled-substances/

43 https://en.wikipedia.org/wiki/Tony_Rice_discography

44 https://www.pegheadnation.com/news-reviews/breaking-news/tony-rice-lessons/

45 https://usdaynews.com/celebrities/tony-rice-death-cause/

46 Tony renders Tom Waits' poignant song, "Pony."

Waits' use of the word "pony" in his song reminds me of its use in the last verse of "I Ride an Old Paint."

Oh when I die, take my saddle from the wall,

Put it on my pony, lead him from his stall.

Tie my bones to his back, turn our faces to the west,
And we'll ride the prairies that we love the best.

bitly link: https://bit.ly/3vpxQ6W

Acknowledgments

My thanks to Sam Bush, Jerry Douglas, Béla Fleck, Frank Poindexter, Ron Rice, Peter Rowan, Mark Schatz, and Harry Sparks for generously sharing their time, stories, and remembrances of Tony.

Thanks as well to Wyatt Rice, Pierre Bensusan, Dick Boak, Tom Diamant, Kari Estrin, Barbara Higbie, Eric Schoenberg, Steve Swan, John Reischman, Mark Johnson, Bill Evans, and Roland White (may he rest in peace), for their thoughts and comments. Thank you Andy DePaul of luthiersupply.com for permission to use the Martin inlay image. Thank you Janet, Julia & Art Dudley, François Robert, Robert Schleifer, Richard Johnston & Frank Ford of Gryphon Stringed Instruments, Laurie Hillis, Todd Gunsher, Vicki Pritchard, and Patrick Ciocca for permission to share their photos. I am grateful to Sunil Sharma for his cover proofs, and to Jerry Zolten, Lorie Karlin, Jerry Douglas, Seth Evans, Dan Miller, and Mark Schatz for critiquing early drafts of the book and/or its cover. I'm indebted to Katie Watts, my editor, for her sharp eyes and purple pen. My sincere thanks to Ama Bolton for her expert, insightful perusal of this document, and her kind words. A special shout out to Ron Rice for his inestimable help, insights and family photos.

Finally, I'm indebted to my wife, Lenona, for standing by me during the creation of this book. Thank you, sweetheart.

Contributors

Pierre Bensusan – Mesmerizing finger-picking DADGAD guitarist, book publisher, and songwriter.

Dick Boak – Artist, writer, woodworker, musician, and long time Martin Guitar employee.

Sam Bush – Hellacious mandolinist, full-throated singer, and founder of progressive bluegrass group, New Grass Revival.

Patrick Ciocca – String and electric bassist, sound consultant, and tour manager of Bill Keith's Bicentennial Bluegrass Band.

Jerry Douglas – Master dobroist, internationally renowned picker, ambassador for acoustic music, and man of big eyes & ears, Jerry is an NEA National Heritage Fellow.

Art Dudley – Writer & *Stereophile* Deputy Editor, Art snapped the shot of the Clarence White Martin on this book's final spread.

Kari Estrin – Tony's agent and manager from roughly 1981 to 1985, and an executive producer on *Me & My Guitar* and one of the *Bluegrass Album Band* albums.

Béla Fleck – Master banjo man of bluegrass to new grass, jazz, rock, and classical music, Béla continues to innovate in the Scruggs-Keith tradition and beyond.

Todd Gunsher – Official photographer for IBMA World of Bluegrass and contributing photographer for *No Depression,* Todd has shot Hornsby, Branford, Steve Martin and, incredibly, Dick Dale.

Barbara Higbie – Bay Area Music Award-winning pianist,

composer, violinist, singer-songwriter, and multi-instrumentalist.

John Holder – Working in the classic tradition of humorous illustration dating to Victorian times, he gives contemporary topics a vintage twist, exemplified by his 1977 Cambridge Festival poster.

Mark Johnson – Creator of Clawgrass, a style of 5-string playing that incorporates bluegrass and clawhammer banjo elements. A longtime Rice family friend, Ron calls Mark, "the fifth Rice brother."

Frank Poindexter – Tony's uncle on his mother's side, singer, and dobroist with Deeper Shade of Blue.

John Reischman – Mandolinist in the first Tony Rice Unit.

Ron Rice – Fellow string bassist, Tony's brother, and guardian of the Tony Rice flame.

Tony Rice – Noted bluegrass and new acoustic music guitarist, singer, tunesmith, songwriter, and bandleader.

Wyatt Rice – Tony's brother, and exceptional bluegrass guitarist.

François Robert – Fine art photographer, received "Best of Fine Art" in the Lucie Awards Competition in 2008.

Peter Rowan – Guitarist, singer, yodeler, songwriter, yarner, *and* genuine "Bluegrass Boy."

Mark Schatz – Bass brother, master of pizz'ed and bowed string bass, clawhammer banjo guy, and bassist in the Tony Rice Unit.

Harry Sparks – Luthier at whose direction Tony restored the Clarence White Martin after it went boating during the 1993 "Storm of the Century" in Florida.

Steve Swan – Owner and operator of Steve Swan String Basses in Burlingame, luthier, bassist, and Tony's housemate for a year.

Roland White – Clarence White's older brother, pioneering bluegrass mandolinist, Bluegrass Boy, and solid sender.

About the Author

Bill Amatneek has been published in *Down Beat, Rolling Stone, Yoga Journal, Storytelling Magazine, Bluegrass Unlimited, Bluegrass Breakdown, Bass World, Musician, Fine Books & Collections*, and anthologized in *Encounters with Bob Dylan: If You See Him Say Hello*. In 2000, his story, "Laying Buddy Down" won a prize in the William Faulkner Writing Competition.

His book, *Acoustic Stories: Pickin' for the Prez and other Unamplified Tales*, was a Foreword Reviews 2013 Silver Book of the Year Award winner in Performing Arts and Music. His 2003 collection, *Acoustic Stories: Playing Bass with Peter, Paul & Mary, Jerry Garcia, and Bill Monroe*, won the Bay Area Independent Publishers Association award for Best Music Book. In 2021, his imprint, Vineyards Press, published *Heart of a Man*, an anthology of men's writings with works by Philip Roth, John Updike, Michael Chabon, Julius Lester, Shakespeare, Andre Dubus III, and 36 others.

He has picked banjo with Frank Wakefield, and Vern & Ray, and string bass with Peter, Paul & Mary, the Greenbriar Boys, Full Faith & Credit Big Band, Peter Rowan and Bill Monroe, Roland White, Keith Little & Jim Nunally, Kathy Kallick, Steve Smith & Hard Road, Jim Hurst, The Bill Brothers (Wild & Mild), Kate Wolf, Mimi Fariña, Bill Keith & the Bicentennial Bluegrass Band, Rowan & Rice, and Eric Bibb. Most recently, he has been heard playing bass with Charlie Garzoli's 17-piece rehearsal band, Jump House, and Doug Adamz' 4-piece belly dance band, Light Rain.

Ordering Discovering Tony Rice

You can order signed copies of *Discovering Tony Rice* at VineyardsPress.com. Signed books are collectible, valuable, and make treasured gifts.

Multinational technology companies, though offering convenient "free" shipping, do not themselves offer signed copies of *Discovering Tony Rice*.

For signed copies, point your browser to VineyardsPress.com, click on Shop, and order away.

The paperback edition of *Discovering Tony Rice* is a first-rate document, well printed, easy to read, and light in weight.

A hardback book is more durable, feels good in your hands, and stands out on your bookshelf – a treasured possession and gift. Some folks say that a book *is* a hardbound book.

You'll be pleased with either edition.

Posting a Review

If you enjoyed reading *Discovering Tony Rice,* and would like to write a review, you can post one on Amazon.

The directions that follow conform to how this website is configured as of February, 2024. By the time you read this, navigation may have drifted.

To post a review on Amazon

1) Direct your browser to Amazon.com, sign into your account, or create a new account if you don't have one.

2) Arriving at the main Amazon page, at the "Search Amazon" prompt, type in "Amatneek." After the Results page displays, and if "Discovering Tony Rice" displays as a live link, click on the book's title to go to its page.

3) Arriving at the book's page, scroll to "Review this product" and underneath it, click on the "Write a customer review" button.

4) Select an Overall Rating of from one to five stars.

5) If you wish, add a headline and/or a photo or video.

6) Add a written review and click on Submit.

L'arte non è
mai finita,
solo
abbandonata.
– DA VINCI

The Clarence White Martin – Photo by Art Dudley
Courtesy of Janet and Julia Dudley

Printed in the USA
CPSIA information can be obtained
at www.ICGtesting.com
CBHW041740150424
6919CB00002B/4

9 781928 578338